WAITING IN THE WINGS

WAITING
····· IN THE ·····
WINGS

How to Launch Your

Performing Career on

Broadway and Beyond

Tiffany Haas

with Jenna Glatzer

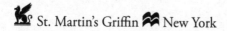 St. Martin's Griffin ✕ New York

WAITING IN THE WINGS. Copyright © 2019 by Tiffany Haas.
All rights reserved. Printed in the United States of America.
For information, address St. Martin's Press,
175 Fifth Avenue, New York, N.Y. 10010.

www.stmartins.com

The Library of Congress Cataloging-in-Publication Data is available
upon request.

ISBN 978-1-250-19373-5 (trade paperback)
ISBN 978-1-250-23239-7 (ebook)

Our books may be purchased in bulk for promotional, educational,
or business use. Please contact your local bookseller or the Macmillan
Corporate and Premium Sales Department at 1-800-221-7945,
extension 5442, or by email at
MacmillanSpecialMarkets@macmillan.com.

First Edition: April 2019

10 9 8 7 6 5 4 3 2 1

To every aspiring performer with a dream.

To my teachers and fellow actors,
thank you for inspiring me.

To my parents,
without whom none of this would be possible.

Contents

A Message to Aspiring Singers, Dancers, and Actors

Do you have a passion for performing? Do you love being on stage? Are you looking to deepen your skill set, feel better prepared for auditions, or gain a better understanding of the industry? Do you want to develop a plan for success as a performer? Then I wrote this book for you.

Passion for what we do runs deep within us as performers and artists! That passion comes with ups and downs, successes and rejections. That's part of what this book is all about.

But there's more to it than simply having a dream and a passion. Real success in this business is about more than singing, dancing, and acting. I want you to learn about some of the most valuable assets you have: **your mind-set, attitude, work ethic, and willingness to do what it takes and never give up!** These are the essential things that set winners apart.

I have been exactly where you are. I want to save you from wasting time on what *doesn't* matter and help you focus on what *does* matter. I am going to tell you my story and my path. It will be different from yours, but the principles and lessons I learned along the way will apply to every successful performer.

A very good friend and fellow Broadway performer once

told young students, "This entire journey must be a joyous one or you will not be successful." That means joy in dreaming, auditioning, training, preparing, and doing the hard work. So, together, let's set big goals, dream big dreams, and make the commitment to work hard and follow through . . . joyously!

—Tiffany Haas

Acknowledgments

A completed book is the culmination of an entire cast coming together. In this cast, there are many I would like to thank and acknowledge for the support I have received throughout this process.

First and foremost thank you to my mom, my dad, and my husband, Stephen, for the constant love, support, and encouragement.

To Jenna Glatzer, who made my thoughts and words come off the page. Thank you for the many long hours, the many laughs, and most of all, thank you for going on this journey with me.

To Michael Flamini, Gwen Hawkes, Sara Ensey, and the editors at St. Martin's Press, thank you for the countless hours reviewing chapters and providing valuable feedback. Thank you to George Witte, Jen Enderlin, and Sally Richardson for your enthusiasm about this book.

To Todd Shuster, Erica Bauman, and Aevitas Management, thank you for your constant support and advice.

I have loved working with you all and thank you all for believing in this book.

To Alan Fischer, Robert Brown, Alice Herring, and Joan Lader, gifted teachers all.

To Michael Rose, Peter Ermides, Donna Vivino, Ernest Richardson, Cesar Rocha, Bobby Logue, Tom Ward, Jennifer Kiesendahl, and Robert Anthony Jones, thank you for your valuable contributions to this book.

Lastly, to all those not individually named, who offered words of wisdom and useful advice, thank you for your tremendous encouragement now and always.

WAITING IN THE WINGS

1

It Took 72 Auditions

There I was in New York City, no longer as a tourist but now a resident. I called my parents after every audition to give them the complete play-by-play—the good and, on this day, the bad.

"I didn't get cast again," I said on the phone through big, heartfelt, blubbery tears. "I think I should come home. It's never going to happen here for me."

It was my third audition since I'd moved. All my life had been in preparation for this—since I was five years old and started putting on impromptu concerts of selections from *Annie* in the living room (red wig and all). Dinner at our house was never just a meal; it was dinner and a show. I knew at a very young age that I loved performing. I had never wanted to do anything else besides make it to New York and be a Broadway star. And now I was finally here in the city that never sleeps, and it was more of a struggle than I'd imagined.

One of my first Broadway auditions was for Belle in *Beauty and the Beast*. I'd read the casting breakdown, and it was just perfect for me; they were looking for a young brunette soprano ingénue type, spunky and charismatic and just my height.

This is me! I thought. *I've got this.* I walked into that building filled to the brim with confidence until the moment I rounded the corner and saw a hundred other young women who looked *exactly like me*. All of a sudden, I realized this was not high school or college with a few people vying for the lead role. This was the real deal where there were literally hundreds of qualified people for *every* role.

There we all were, young brunette soprano ingénues, all holding our books of sheet music, all wearing flowing dresses. I got my first reality check. This is something we all know about before moving to NYC. We hear the stories about thousands of people waiting to be seen, or lines wrapped around a building for an audition, but when you see it with your own eyes, it hits you in the face! I had a moment where I thought, *Huh, so those stories are true.*

I knew the real world of professional theatre was going to be competitive, but until I stood in that hallway surrounded by talented women, I didn't realize *how* competitive. I had no idea how I would ever stand out, and in the end, I didn't—I didn't even get a callback for the role I was so sure was meant to be mine.

"Listen," my dad said. "You have three people involved in this career, and two of us are not worried. Keep going."

It was a blessing I knew not everyone had—two supportive parents who never once told me that I should have a fallback career. (You'll get their take on things later on in the book.) They believed in me more than I believed in myself at times, and they reminded me to persevere, stay committed, and move on to the next audition. And so I did!

Seventy-two of them, in fact, before my big break.

There are lots of ways to get into a performing career, but I come at it with my own life experiences and biases about what worked for me. We are all different, but the lessons I learned are applicable to anyone determined to succeed.

My Path to Broadway: Early Lessons Learned

New York City was a long way from my home in Virginia, and a much different atmosphere. I grew up in my mother's dance studio, Academy of Dance. I began taking classes at the age of three and spent much of my childhood training as a competitive dancer, but I loved to sing just as much. My mom had a clear understanding of the dance world, but the singing world was new to all of us. Finding someone who would teach voice lessons to an eight-year-old was certainly a challenge. My mom had a dear friend who was a highly accomplished voice teacher, a former Miss Alabama and a true Southern belle who wore shoulder pads with *everything*. She didn't teach children under the age of twelve, so my mom asked her to meet with me one time as a personal favor. When the lesson ended, I ran out to my mom's car with a handwritten note. (No cell phones or texting at that time.)

The note read:

The Virginia Opera is holding auditions for its children's chorus this week and Tiffany needs to audition.

The next day, my mom drove me to Norfolk, where I auditioned for the Virginia Opera children's chorus. I was accepted, and that turned out to be where I got my first taste of professional performing. It's also where I found a love of opera and classical music. We performed *La Bohème,* and a six-foot-five flamboyant man who looked like a black version of Arnold Schwarzenegger was cast as my father. I loved it! That wonderful man soon played a very important role in my life.

Starting when I was about ten, I convinced my mother to get me an agent and take me to TV, film, and theatre auditions. We traveled to New York without my dad even knowing sometimes.

One time, we were on the train going over my lines and my dad called. My mother picked up nervously. "Hello?"

"Hi, honey. Do you want to meet for lunch?"

"Well, um . . ."

"Where are you girls?"

"New York?"

They were a funny balance. My mom was the one who was more spontaneous and creative, and my dad was more practical. He was always supportive, but he didn't want me missing school. I had a final callback for *Interview with the Vampire,* and he wouldn't allow me to go because it meant I would miss the first day of school. I was a wreck about it.

"This is the biggest moment of my life!" I protested.

"The first day of school is the biggest moment of your life, not an audition."

I can understand and agree with the wisdom of his words now, but it felt like the end of the world at the time, and I dropped to my knees and cried just like a proper little actress.

When I got to middle school and my parents sent me to a private prep school, I floundered and felt like I wasn't fitting in. All my parents wanted was to give me the best education possible so that I'd be able to go to whatever college I wanted, like my dad, a West Point grad and financial advisor.

The headmistress (a wonderful woman) did me a big favor when she took my father aside and said, "Have you ever used calculus again in your life after school?"

"Never, really," my father said.

"Neither will she, and she doesn't want to be a financial advisor. Get her out of this school and put her somewhere she can really thrive and do what she loves."

It was a shock to my parents to hear such a thing, but they took it to heart. What I loved was performing, and where I belonged was a performing arts school. So in a decision that would change my life, my parents switched gears and put me exactly where I needed to be and where I would thrive . . . the Governor's School for the Arts. Looking back, I realize this was a huge sacrifice for my parents because they spent almost three hours a day driving to make this happen!

A great lesson here: There are people who will come into your life and help you along the way. Listen to them. Learn from them.

High School (the Governor's School)

Admission to the Governor's School was by audition only. It was a public school, but you still had to be selected based on your audition. All around me was an eclectic mix of kids—some coming from privileged families; some who had very difficult home lives and no solid parental figures. But we all had something in common: We loved to perform.

I wasn't sure whether I'd major in voice, musical theatre, or dance. I picked the Judy Garland song "Get Happy" and gave it my all. I tried so hard to passionately imitate Judy's famous swoons and croons. Really? A Judy Garland song, and I was going from eighth grade to ninth grade! Pretty funny as I think back on that choice today, but I wanted this at fourteen years old, and I was fearless.

After my audition, two men—one of whom turned out to be the man who had played my father in *La Bohème*—followed us out to the car.

"I would love to work with you and help you develop your voice," the other man said. His name was Alan Fischer, and he would soon become my mentor, voice teacher, and dear friend. "She needs to develop her voice classically. It's where her voice lives. We want to work with her. After she develops classically, she'll be able to sing anything she wants, but please consider our program."

We were amazed that they had bothered to chase us out to the car, and we figured that anyone who showed that much enthusiasm about me probably should be my teacher. And it was a great move—those two men were partners in the program, and they made a phenomenal team. They were my teammates, like two uncles who shaped me as a musician and a performer.

Robert Brown was the big guy from *La Bohème,* hilariously larger-than-life and expressive. He spit when he spoke, and when my classmates and I would complain, "Mr. Brown, you spit on me!" he would say with his famous drawl, "It's good for your complexion, baby!" And Alan Fischer encouraged us to push our own limits. He challenged us with material that many teachers would never consider for high schoolers. But he believed that we were capable of anything. Even as high schoolers, he immersed us in the world of music and treated us as young professionals. He took us to New York City, introduced us to his colleagues—professional opera singers like Plácido Domingo, Renée Fleming, and Denyce Graves.

There are many performing arts high schools throughout the country, as well as state governor's school programs. In regards to Virginia's program, I went to my normal high school (the public high school I was zoned for) in the morning to take my core classes (English, math, social studies, and the like) and then took a bus to the Governor's School in the afternoon. We got out later than public schools—my last class ended at 5:00 p.m. If there were rehearsals for school shows, I stayed until 9:00 p.m. If not, I went to my dance classes at my mom's studio each night.

For my parents, the driving game and sacrifice had just begun. For me, it meant, among other things, that I couldn't really participate in after-school activities with my friends. Most of my high school girlfriends were cheerleaders, and I really wanted to be with them and wear the cute uniform and the adorable high ponytail with a bow like they did, but I couldn't make the rehearsals. Finally, they helped me wrangle a spot as the mascot so I could at least travel to games with them.

(There was a slight bit of confusion when I tried to put my own touch on the mascot . . . I put a big bow on the bear's ears to make her look girly when I carried the game ball at homecoming. The football players were furious! "You're not one of the girls! You're supposed to be a scary bear!")

I also didn't get to do most of my high school musicals (because I was doing shows at the Governor's School), even though I really wanted to. It was hard knowing that my friends were doing things together without me, but at a young age, I was learning the meaning of making choices and sacrifices for what I wanted.

After our four years in the Governor's School vocal program, Mr. Fischer did something amazing: He made it part of our last day to go back and watch our original audition tapes. We all got to laugh and see how far we'd come in our time there. It's funny looking back now, because I was so sure and confident of that audition, but after those years of training, I giggled watching the tape. We all did! It was amazing how much I had grown and learned in high school. Without the help and guidance of Alan Fischer and Robert Brown, I never would have been prepared for college auditions or succeeded in professional theatre. It's amazing what happens when someone believes in you!

And it didn't just happen to me. Soon after I graduated, a boy named Ryan Speedo Green arrived. He had grown up in a trailer park and later in a bullet-ridden shack and was in seclusion in juvenile hall at the age of twelve for making threats.

He was angry and had a tough background to overcome—but he also had tremendous raw talent. After training with Mr. Brown and Mr. Fischer, Ryan went on to win the 2011 Metropolitan Opera National Council Auditions and is now a professional opera singer performing all over the world.

VALUE YOUR SUPPORTERS

There will be sacrifices and a price to pay for anything worthwhile, but there will be people in your life who are rooting for you and who will help you. Make sure you appreciate them. Success for a young performing artist definitely requires a support system. Whether your support system is your parents or a Robert Brown, success in the performing arts is not a do-it-yourself project.

College: More Training and More Lessons Learned

There are many paths to success. I decided to continue my training after high school by attending an opera/musical theatre program in college. My parents and I selected five or six schools that seemed to be a good fit and planned our trips to visit the schools and prepare to audition. If this is your path, do your homework! Schools are different; they have varying requirements for admission, and you'll need to plan your trips to each school you are interested in.

It's very, very different from the college admissions process if you want to be an engineer, a biologist, or a lawyer, or you just haven't decided. Most times, you'll need to apply to the school or university *and* the musical theatre program within the school itself. You'll need to audition for them as well. Find out exactly what they want, prepare and prepare, and be ready to present your years of study in one song or one dance combination, or one monologue! Ask what they want. They are all different.

This becomes a bit of a family project and one you should get started on as a junior if possible. Then you'll be ready for auditions during your senior year.

Visit the schools you are interested in. Try to decide if this is the place you'll want to spend four years of your life. Do you want to go to a small conservatory in a small town? That will certainly be a different four years from attending a huge school like NYU and living in New York City. I auditioned for five schools during the fall and winter of my senior year.

My choice was the University of Cincinnati College–Conservatory of Music (CCM), one of the country's top-ranking music schools. I initially began as an opera major and eventually switched to musical theatre along with an intimate group of up-and-comers. Let me be very straightforward here and say that you *do not* need this type of education to wind up on Broadway—there are many paths. One time after a performance of *Wicked* during a Q&A session, an audience member asked each of my fellow cast members, "Could you each tell us which conservatory you went to?" and I was one of the few cast members who actually went to a conservatory. One of my friends never went to college; she showed up in New York straight from high school. Another was a political science major at a liberal arts school. There's no checkbox on the résumé to make sure you went to a prestigious music or theatre program in college.

But the one thing that we all had in common was the *training*. Regardless of our individual paths to Broadway, we all spent hundreds of hours in dance studios, voice lessons, and acting classes—not to mention hearing *no* at auditions and learning to go again and keep persevering! A musical theatre program is all about training and preparation for eventually auditioning to get a job. If you don't go to a program like this after high school, remember that you'll be competing for that job with plenty of talented young performers who have spent four years in a rigorous program of preparation. They, too, will have spent hundreds of hours in dance studios, voice lessons, and acting classes. They will have years of mock audition experience. They will have competed for parts in shows while in school and heard *no* many times. That's your competition. That said, there are no guarantees. Whoever brings it to the audition room generally gets the job.

There are, however, several advantages to a conservatory or musical theatre school. First, of course, is the education itself—you'll be immersed in music and acting in ways that were never possible before. This may be the first and only opportunity you'll get to completely focus on honing your skills as a performer before getting out there into the giant question mark of your career. Not only that, but you are learning accountability. Mom and Dad aren't there to be sure you're waking up for school. They're not there to bring you your dance bag if you forgot it.

But aside from the training, there's another major benefit to conservatories in recent years: *the showcase*.

Showcase Season

This is becoming more and more popular with college programs: Each spring, college programs like CCM's host a showcase in New York City (and sometimes Los Angeles) during spring of senior year to highlight all or some of their graduating seniors. At some schools, you have to audition to get a spot in the showcase, but most of them are for any senior who wants to participate. (At CCM, we were each given time to perform and show off our best material at a rented space.) Numerous casting directors, agents, managers, choreographers, producers, and directors come to these events to see the newest talent. It's even known as "showcase season," and industry pros know to keep their schedules open for as many of them as possible. It's where they scope out new talent from around the country and try to grab the most promising people for their agencies or their shows.

My showcase was tremendously productive for me. Roughly eight to ten talent agents and managers were interested in meeting me and left their contact information. I immediately set out to meet with them all to see if *we* would be a good fit. I signed with one agency, and things began to get busy fast. The week after my showcase filled up quickly with appointments and auditions thanks to the connections I made there. As a matter of fact, I even received a job offer at the showcase. There was a gentleman in attendance who was directing *Hello, Dolly!* in Kansas City. He said, "I just had a girl drop out. She's a high soprano in the ensemble. Can you do it? It leaves in a couple of weeks." It was an Equity regional theatre; I gladly said yes, and this is how I got my Equity card (we'll get into the pros and cons of the labor union Actors' Equity Association in chapter 11). Bottom line, the showcase is a tremendous opportunity and wonderful introduction to NYC and the industry. Otherwise, you arrive in NYC (a place flooded with talent) with your suitcase and your fingers crossed.

There are other showcase opportunities that have cropped up, too. Someone rents a space, hires an accompanist, and collects fees from any performers who want to appear. It's not something attended by industry professionals unless the organizer is paying them to be there. Be wary of spending your money to perform.

So the lesson here is this: When you are considering college choices, ask if they have a showcase in New York for seniors. It will give you an opportunity to quickly get connected with people who can help you!

So You're in NYC . . . Now What?

I officially moved to New York in May of 2005 following the showcase at the end of my senior year. If I ever thought that my life was going to be smooth sailing because I had an agent, that notion was quickly dispelled. Having representation is wonderful, oftentimes crucial for getting to the next level in your career; however, don't assume that having an agent means you can now sit back and relax. It's a team effort, and the team captain is *you*. You must still stay invested in your own career; look for opportunities, and know that your agent is doing the same. My agent did set me up with appointments, but very few casting directors wanted to see me for one simple reason: There are eleventy billion actors in New York and no one knew who I was.

Okay, okay, I might be *slightly* exaggerating. Eleventy million.

The thing is, casting professionals have a limited amount of time at each audition. They want to see the best of the best, get their show cast as quickly as they can, and move on to rehearsals or casting the next show on their list. In the case of a new Broadway show, the audition process may take a few weeks: first the open auditions, then callbacks, then potentially several more rounds of callbacks to match people up—for example, they might want to see how the female lead looks next to the male lead (is he too short, or is she too tall?), or what kind of chemistry the "best friends" have when they read together. So as one role is cast, others may be rearranged to fit. But it can't all go on indefinitely; someone is paying for the audition space and the director's time, and there is a show date that needs to be met. So by necessity, even if a casting director had unlimited patience, he can't see all the people in the world who want to audition.

This is a major way it's different from high school, college, and community theatre. Usually at that level, anyone who wants to audition gets to audition. All you have to do is show up and probably sit in the auditorium and listen to everyone else. You may even get to sing an entire song, regardless of whether or not you can sing. Not so in professional theatre. If you're lucky enough to get seen, you're expected to sing just a portion of the song (and possibly other songs, if the casting director likes what he hears) in a private space with the casting professionals, make a big impression, and then make way for the next person.

There are two ways to audition for a Broadway show: at an open call, or by appointment.

Open Call Auditions

Open calls for Broadway shows are massive, the lines often stretch down the block outside, and there's no guarantee that you'll get seen. When you are a non-Equity actor, you are given last priority. If there's any time left at the end after all the Equity people have been seen, then you get your shot. But you could spend your entire day just sitting in line, waiting and hoping, only to leave without ever singing or dancing.

The calls for musicals are usually split into singer and dancer calls, even though you really need both skills. But most people have one skill that's stronger than others, so you highlight that. You might be a "singer who dances," or in the lesser form, a "singer who moves well" or "moves very well." Conversely, you might be a "dancer who sings" or an "actor who sings." For example, the understudies for the leading (singer) roles are often dancing their butts off in ensemble each night. So if you're a "singer only," start taking ballet now!

Open calls can be overwhelming. When *Hair* held a non-Equity casting call in 2010 after the original Broadway cast moved to London, actors were already lining up at 1:00 a.m. outside the theatre—in freezing-cold *January* in *New York,* and two casting directors split up into two different rooms in the hopes of seeing seven hundred people in one day. The brand-new cast debuted in March.

When more people show up for an open call than expected, or just when it's getting near the end of the day and there are still lots of people remaining to be seen, you may get even less time than you had anticipated. Normally, they ask you to prepare a sixteen- or thirty-two-bar cut of a song, but I've seen auditions where the casting director peeks his or her head out of the room to announce that there's only time for eight bars. Eight bars! That's nothing! At that point, they're just trying to weed out the numbers to something more manageable for callbacks. All they can really learn in eight bars is whether you can sing at all and what you look like, but it's certainly enough to decide whether they want to see more. Frankly, when you've been sitting behind a table for hours at a time, eight bars can be plenty!

It's just another reason to get to open calls early. Since you're normally seen in the order you arrive, you want to have every possible chance of 1) being seen, and 2) having time to sing your full cut. The later you arrive, the lower your chances are of even getting a slot. Try to arrive an hour before call time.

This takes discipline. This takes perseverance. This is *not* for someone easily discouraged. Auditions start early, and maybe you were out late the night before. But acting is a job, and auditioning is part of the job, so think of it as an early shift. When you know you have an early audition, have the discipline to go to bed early the night before and wake up with plenty of time to have a good breakfast and get warmed up for the audition. And, though it should go without saying, *be prepared*. Know your material. Your competition will know the material!

WHERE TO FIND OPEN CALLS

• ***Backstage* magazine and Backstage.com:** This long-running industry favorite lists casting calls from all over the country, including Broadway, regional, cruise lines, cabarets, theme parks, and more. You can even look at their audition calendar to see which auditions are happening on what days; a recent random Tuesday had thirty-four auditions listed. You can browse for free, but you have to pay for a subscription to get full details.

• **Projectcasting.com:** This one focuses on television and film, with frequent calls for extras and speaking roles in commercials, documentaries, pilots, TV and web series, and so on. It contains listings in many major cities across the United States and is free.

• **Playbill.com/jobs:** This Broadway staple has its own website with a free casting and job listings section. It's great to find not only casting calls for plays but also other jobs performers may want—like musical theatre camp directors. It's updated daily with listings for New York and regional theatres across the country, and it includes pay rates and requirements.

• **AuditionsFree.com:** This free website lists nationwide casting calls for film, TV, stage, theme parks, web series, and more. You can search by geographic area and sign up for emailed notices. You don't need to make an account to get full information.

- **ActorsAccess.com:** You or your agent can put up your headshot and résumé and a reel here and find listings by city for theatre, film, internet, music videos, staged readings, and more, both union and nonunion. There are many projects listed here every day, and they all look at online submissions.

- **OneonOneNYC.com:** This company focuses on workshops taught by casting directors in NYC and LA. There is a membership fee, and you'll have to audition to become a member, but you'll get the opportunity to meet industry pros who you'd probably never get to talk to otherwise and receive access to some casting information that's not openly posted.

- **ActorsEquity.org:** When you're a member, you can log onto the website and find casting calls there as well.

Appointment Auditions

Of course, it's a lot more pleasant to get an appointment for an audition than it is to show up at an open call. Appointments may go through your agent or someone else you've worked with who's associated with the production. In that case, you'll have instructions about where to be, a specific time slot, what to bring, what role you're auditioning for, and any other relevant information. Agents often get a lot more information than performers do, which is one of the many things that make them valuable. Plus, you won't need to get in line at 6:00 a.m. for an audition that starts at 9:00 a.m.!

It should be obvious that you should show up early for your appointment and be really, really prepared . . . and yet people blow it all the time by *not* being prepared and showing up with excuses. They could be perfect for the role, but they didn't prepare the material as well as they should have, and it was a missed opportunity. Even if you're not right for that exact role, when you work hard and prepare the material, you will still make a great impression and perhaps you're right for something else they're casting.

When you get the script or music ahead of time, learn the material! Know it as if you were prepped for the first day of rehearsal. Oftentimes, you are asked to prepare a song or two from the show as well as a couple of scenes from the show, known as *sides*. Sometimes you don't have much notice and time to prepare for the audition, so do the best you can and try to know that material as well as you can. When you're given material from the creative team to prepare for the audition, it is not expected that you'll have it memorized. However, if you are completely glued to the paper, there is no way for you really to connect with the material and present it. Our job is to lift the story off the page! A huge benefit to getting an appointment audition through an agent is that you're able to actually prepare material from that particular show and you have the opportunity to show the creative team what you would do with the role if you got the part.

The job of an actor is not just performing in a show. It's also showing up at auditions, pounding the pavement, getting your foot in the door, taking classes, preparing songs and sides, and putting yourself in the material. It is a fact that you will hear *no* more times than you hear *yes,* and that's okay. Preparing for auditions takes a lot of work. It can often feel like wasted time when you spend hours on the material, learning and coaching the songs and scenes, and you hear, "Thank you. That's all we need to see today." But remember, it's not wasted time . . . it's part of the job!

You have one precious thing that is all yours: your reputation. Your preparedness, your attitude, your willingness to try new things, and your enthusiasm are all things that make up your reputation. Auditioning is hard work and tough on the ego. Remember, casting people, directors, dance captains, and everyone involved in a show are looking at you as a potential employee and a member of a tightly knit cast. Nobody wants to risk their show and spend their time with an unprepared actor who is not pleasant and who will be difficult to work with. During a Q&A with some audience members, I was once asked, "What's it like to work with all the *divas* on Broadway?" My answer was "I don't know" because they really don't last! Enough said.

Speaking of that, let me tell you what it's really like to work on a Broadway show.

2

Life on Broadway

Here's something that really shocks people about making the transition from amateur to professional theatre: You have a *lot* less time to prepare. This is show business, and as a business, time is money.

In high school, you probably have at least two or three months of after-school practices before you perform. On Broadway, you get about two weeks of full days (mine were from about 10:00 a.m. to 5:00 p.m.) when you're a replacement to the show. And it's not even with the cast.

(Huh? Two weeks without the cast?) Yeah! I actually had no idea what was coming until I showed up for my first *Wicked* rehearsal at the Gershwin Theatre.

Here's how it generally works. Unless you have the opportunity to work on a new show from the ground up and you have the exciting opportunity of being a part of the original cast of a new Broadway show, you are actually hired as a replacement in a Broadway show. There is only one original cast, and once their contracts expire—or any of them leave to do something else—then replacements are needed. This happens frequently in every show that lasts for more than a few months. For instance, take a major show that lasts years and figure that your principal (lead) characters will be replaced about every nine months (depending on that show's contract), and the ensemble roles, understudies, and swings will be replaced whenever those people *choose* to leave (e.g., whether it's for a different show, a medical leave, a move away, or for any of a variety of reasons). Members of the ensemble are typically on an open-ended contract. There is a lot of turnover in a long-running show.

So probably 90 percent of the time, you're being hired to take over in an already-running show. You will certainly get more than two weeks if you're in the original cast and everything is being set for the first time, but if you're a replacement, here's how it normally works: You will first learn your music with someone from the music department (an associate music director or a rehearsal pianist), then you come in every day and rehearse your staging and choreography with two people—the dance captain and stage manager. In order to make this a successful process, *come prepared*! You will get the script ahead of time. Learn your material, your lines, and show up ready to work. It's difficult to learn the staging and choreography elements if you are glued to your script.

Then you watch every performance of the show during those two weeks to study your part. You may also "trail" the show backstage, which means to trail the actor you are replacing. This gives you an opportunity to see their onstage choreography and staging from the wings as well as their off-stage choreography—meaning their backstage traffic and quick changes. Having the backstage perspective is especially helpful and totally necessary when you're learning the timing of a show.

But that's right—you do not rehearse with the cast or the orchestra. They've already been playing these roles for months or years, and they do not need to rehearse anymore. They're not going to waste their days coming in to practice every time someone new shows up, and there is no budget to pay them all to do so.

Understand that commercial theatre is a business, and even as much as it's about art and culture and wonderfulness, it's also driven by a bottom line. If a show isn't profitable, it ends, so they want to pay performers as little as possible to rehearse; you're getting paid for those two weeks of rehearsal time, but not more than that because that eats into the budget. Sometimes, when someone needs to be replaced immediately because of an emergency, they want someone who can learn it even quicker.

At the end of your short practice period, you get one rehearsal with the cast, called a *put-in,* on the day before your first performance. You are in full dress (costume), but the other performers are in their street clothes. It is likely the first time you are meeting many of them. You may have a romantic scene to play with one of them the following night, or a comedic scene that relies on your timing, and this is the first time you've ever laid eyes on each other. I remember my Broadway put-in as if it were yesterday. I kept introducing myself to cast members who I had already met, but that's because I had met them when I was backstage trailing. I had met them in wigs and costume and didn't recognize anyone in their normal street clothes. However, I was relieved months later when it was another actor's put-in and he introduced himself to me numerous times . . . in each of my different costumes. Ha!

Because of this revolving door of performers, and because lighting, sound, and automation cues are all so precise, you don't get the creative license to move around the stage as you feel inspired to do so. A long-running show is like a well-oiled machine. Not only that, but in a long-running show, you might have more than just cast swings or understudies on stage; you might have crew subs or crew understudies as well, so there isn't much room to take liberties with a role that has already been created. You can certainly *color* a role a little differently from the last person, which is to be expected since you are a different person, but you still need to stay within the lines.

The director isn't around regularly after the show is set; once it's running, you'll get most of your notes from the stage manager and dance captain. Unlike in community theatre, the stage managers on Broadway and national tours are in charge of the whole production; they take notes from the director in the beginning and make sure the show stays on track with the original vision.

Joining *Wicked* . . . After Seven Tries

Glinda became a dream role the moment I saw *Wicked*. It was a role I just knew I was born to play. My senior year at CCM, a friend and I decided to take a weekend and go to NYC to see the show. I remember exactly where I was sitting in the audience of the Gershwin Theatre. The lights came up at intermission, and I couldn't move. I had never been affected by a show in such a way. I remember my friend saying, "Tiff, that role is you!" Upon graduation and showcase, I wasn't expecting a lead role right out of the gate, of course, but it was something I hoped to work toward. And so I auditioned for *Wicked* . . . seven times.

Yep, seven separate casting calls and appointments. Sometimes they were looking for a Glinda standby, a Glinda understudy, a Nessarose cover, a Glinda *and* Nessa cover all in one . . . They said encouraging things from time to time that let me know they remembered me, but six times in a row, they didn't cast me, and I was about ready to give up.

I was in San José doing regional theatre when I got a call saying they wanted me to come back and audition again.

I called my parents.

"The cost of the plane ticket to New York and back is going to be what I'm making on this job. This is ridiculous. I don't think I'm going to waste the money. They've already seen me six times. What's going to be different about this time?"

My mom said, "You just never know, Tiffany. You can't give up."

She's the dreamer, so that's about what I expected her to say, but my dad pushed it over the edge. "I'll never win the lottery because I don't play it. You need to buy a plane ticket."

I did. That time, they were casting for an immediate replacement in the ensemble who also covered a principal role, and at the end of the call, they sent me to the wardrobe department to try on costumes. They didn't say anything about my getting the part, though.

Could it be that this is such an emergency that they'll only cast someone who fits the costumes? I wondered.

Two members of the wardrobe department tucked and pinned the costumes around me. I hoped it was a good sign that they were fitting the costumes to me like this, but the casting people still stayed straight-faced, not letting on whether they were doing this with several auditioners or just me.

When my agent called the next morning, I could barely breathe.

"Tiffany, you got it! You're going to be on Broadway!"

It was everything I had dreamed of. Finally, after seventy-two auditions, it was happening. Mind you, seventy-two auditions sounds like a lot (it is); however, all those auditions were in five months' time. So it goes to show that auditioning really becomes a full-time job.

"You've been cast as a swing! You're making your Broadway debut!"

I didn't ask a lot of questions during that conversation, but I immediately called my parents and yelled into the phone.

"Who are you playing?" they asked me.

"Swing! I'm playing a girl named Swing!"

Wow, I had definitely missed the ball there! I didn't exactly know what a *swing* was. I initially thought that was my character's name! Well, it kind of was . . . and I quickly learned the value of the position. In fact, a *swing* is a person who covers many of the ensemble roles; in my case, it meant that I would learn the female ensemble tracks as well as understudy a principal role so that I could fill in for any one of them on any given night. If the Elphaba understudy went on as Elphaba, then I went on in her ensemble track, or if someone was hurt in the middle of the show, I needed to jump in the show as soon as possible and take over.

Growing up in a dance studio really helped with this position. I was always able to pick up combinations quickly and confidently—that's an important skill in auditions and when you need to learn multiple tracks in a show and keep them all straight.

Swings are the first line of backups for the ensemble. If someone calls in sick, has a vacation or personal day, or even gets injured in the middle of the show, we're sent in. We get blueprints of the stage marked out with each of our tracks—numbered to show where each actor stands in each scene or dance number and where the set pieces are.

Understudies, on the other hand, are in the ensemble and are occasionally sent in to play lead roles. (Then a swing takes over for their ensemble role.) Sometimes you can be both a swing and an understudy and get paid extra. Finally, there are standbys for some lead roles. Standbys aren't in the show; they're in the theatre waiting in case they're needed. They're the first line of defense if a principal calls in sick; understudies are the second.

My Broadway debut was so thrilling to me. Ben Vereen was playing the Wizard! I was stepping in for the "midwife track"—the track that delivers the green baby in the beginning of the show, performs throughout the ensemble, and operates the Oz Head. (The latter was one of my favorite things to do!) Immediately following "One Short Day," the giant and majestic Oz Head moves downstage to a powerful musical interlude—something that has *grand entrance* written all over it. This particular track had to exit the stage a little early during "One Short Day" to get behind the Oz Head before it's revealed. Three people needed to be behind it: the Wizard, the Oz Head operator, and a stage manager. It was a tight space, and the best way to move downstage with the Oz Head and not be seen by the audience was to step up on the platform behind the head and hold on to the rails and ride it downstage. So Ben Vereen, the stage manager, and I would stand side by side with our toes on the platform, heels hanging off, hands on the sides, and ride downstage to the powerful Oz. The orchestra was underneath the stage, and in this moment, I could feel the vibration of the bass and drums throughout my entire body! It was such a magical theatrical moment.

Knowing it was my Broadway debut, Ben Vereen looked at me during our ride downstage, held on with one hand, hung off the back like he was Gene Kelly in that famous moment in *Singin' in the Rain* when he swings around the pole, and yelled with great enthusiasm, "Woo-hoo! Welcome to Oz, baby!" Ha! I will never forget it.

At the end of the show, the ensemble members all bow in two lines (men and women) behind the principals, but on that day, one of my castmates and fellow swings (who was also on for an ensemble track that day) pushed me to the front of the stage, and I received flowers in front of the audience.

It was such a special extra treat from the stage manager, who loved to recognize people making their Broadway debuts or on their last day of the show.

Then it was over. I would never make my Broadway debut again. It was strange; it was so earth-shatteringly huge, but only to me. The rest of the cast had already been there and done that, so it was just another night to them. I went to sleep that night so thankful, so excited, but already wondering, *What next?* Now that I had achieved my biggest life goal, where would I go from there?

In the beginning, I didn't know what my job would be like or how often I'd go on, but it turned out that I performed in almost every show. There was nearly always someone out sick, taking a vacation or a personal day, or needing a break for one reason or another. I very quickly learned every inch of that show backward and forward. I could have jumped in for the Wizard and Madame Morrible, too!

Once I went on in the middle of the show because someone fell. Another time, I was already on stage performing one role and someone else had to drop out, so they switched me to her role and had a different swing take over the role I was doing.

"We're really swinging now!" she said to me.

Later, I was cast as Glinda's standby, and I remember a time when I was hanging out backstage painting my nails with the Elphaba standby, and suddenly the stage manager said, "Get yourself together! You're going on."

I didn't even have my makeup on. In a mad rush, someone was hooking my bra and pulling my dress up, someone else was putting on my wig, another person was clipping on my mic, and minutes later, I was on stage thinking, *Where am I?* You have to stay vocally warmed up, but we weren't required to be ready for the stage until we got the notice we were going on. It's hilarious to me looking back on it now, but at the time, I found nothing funny about it. It was scary to realize I could have that little warning.

What It's Like Being a Broadway Performer

So let me give you the scoop about life as a Broadway performer.

The two main things you need to understand are: 1) it is awesome, and 2) it is repetitive. Being on Broadway is a dream, and for so many of us it represents something big— it means we've *made it.* We were chosen out of thousands and thousands of people who wanted the role, and we learned the part and got on that stage and made it through and got to feel what it was like to take a bow *on Broadway.* It's huge, it really is. Big stars have emerged from there, while others happily work for decades without any real name recognition but with the satisfaction of sustaining a high-level career as a performer.

The pay is good, too. The Actors' Equity Association ("Actors' Equity") sets the minimum acceptable rates, which you can find in the document library section of www.actors equity.org. As of this writing, the minimum weekly salary for a Broadway ensemble member is about $1,900, plus extra for any additional responsibilities you have—for instance, you get paid extra each week for being an understudy, for each role you swing, for being a dance captain, and so on. You also get extra for any hazards involved—for example, if you have to do a stunt or if there's a raked stage (a stage that slants upward as you move upstage so the audience gets a better view—which can be very hard on your body and challenging to dance on).

Principal actors (lead roles) not only are on a different pay scale but a different contract entirely; ensemble actors have open-ended contracts, so they can stay as long as they want once they pass a six-month probationary period where either party can cancel the contract if it's not working out, whereas principals are cast for a specific time slot that can be re-newed if the producers choose to make that offer. As an en-semble member, you can choose to stay with a show for years and years if you want to . . . and as long as the show stays open.

But it can be hard to imagine what it is like to perform exactly the same show eight times a week for months or years. In high school and college, you work for weeks and weeks preparing and growing in anticipation of opening night, and you do one or two exciting weekends and then it's over. In community theatre, you might do a few weekends. On Broadway, it's eight shows a week. And it's the same every night. The same songs, same lines, same choreography, hit-ting the same spots on the stage at the same moment, same costumes, same everything. All that differs is the audience—and it needs to be fresh and energetic for them every time. For many of the audience members, it's the first time they've ever seen a Broadway show. The job of an actor in a long-running show is to have consistency on stage while still being authentic and staying in the moment. An audience (with trained eyes or not) can feel whether or not a per-former is being genuine and authentic. You have to look freshly surprised at that line you've said 125 times already, and your eyes have to sparkle during that song you just sang at the matinée.

By necessity, you have to say your lines with just the same timing night after night or you can mess up the technical cues. You're likely to hear afterward from the stage manager that taking an extra pause because you're trying to "keep it fresh" or do something creative threw off the timing for the sound or lighting, so you'll be told to stick to the same way you've done it all along (unless you get special permission from the director to do it differently).

Performing on Broadway is a full-time job, and your body is your tool. One of my stage managers always reminded us that just as many people start their workdays at 8:00 a.m., we have to remember that our workday begins at about 7:00 p.m. So you can't run yourself ragged all day and show up to the theatre tired . . . just when you are supposed to *begin* your workday.

Living in New York

If you don't already live in New York City, obviously you'll need to move there if your dream is to perform on Broadway. New York is different from any other city on Earth. It has its own energy and culture, and not everyone can be happy living there.

It's also very expensive to live in New York. Rent is high (average is over $2,300 for a studio apartment, though many actors share apartments), and space is very limited. Don't expect sprawling living space unless you're independently wealthy. I have a friend in her late thirties who has six roommates. I wouldn't want that, but she's perfectly happy that way. It's all about what works for you.

I found my apartment on Craigslist in 2005, but if I were to do it over today, I'd go to the popular audition studios instead. They all have bulletin boards inside where people post notices, and one of the things often posted is apartment listings. You'll often see notices for apartments that are available for a six- or twelve-month term; those are sublets from actors who have been hired for tours, cruises, or out-of-town jobs. There's a lot of turnover. Actors know what other actors can afford, so most of the rent costs on these boards are less than what you'll find elsewhere. On these boards, you can also find photographers advertising their headshot services, voice coaches, web designers, and whatever else you might need.

You can also find apartments on a Facebook group called Ghostlight Housing, which focuses exclusively on people in the performing arts in New York City. You can post if you're looking for a place, looking for roommates, or if you have a place to sublet.

Winters are rough. So many times, I walked through heavy snow to get into the theatre, thinking, *Who's going to show up? How are they going to get here?* but Broadway nearly never closes. There could be a state of emergency, and it would say, "No one leave your house unless you're an emergency worker . . . or a Broadway actor."

The city is loud, traffic is terrible, and the daily routines you may be used to in a small town will be drastically different there. You won't be driving your car to the grocery store in NYC. You'll most likely be walking. I will never forget walking out of the grocery store with two large (and very heavy) paper bags of groceries into a rainstorm that had started while I was inside. I didn't have an umbrella, but I lived so close to this particular store that I figured I could just deal with it and go quickly. But the rain dampened the paper bags so badly that one completely split at the bottom and my groceries fell onto the sidewalk. FYI: The five-second rule does *not* apply to the sidewalks of NYC. Just leave it in the trash and walk away! Trust me on that!

The lesson here is not "Bring an umbrella with you everywhere you go" . . . the lesson is that things will be different in NYC, and you have to learn to go with the flow and deal with it. Keep your head high, and don't sweat the small stuff. When you need to get somewhere quickly, it can feel like the subway train you need is always out of service and there are no cabs in sight, and after a rainstorm, the trash cans of the city are filled with defeated umbrellas that didn't survive the storm.

However, NYC also has its own magic that's completely indescribable. When I walk the streets of New York, I can't help but hear the Jay-Z and Alicia Keys song "Empire State of Mind" playing in my head: "These streets will make you feel brand new; big lights will inspire you."

You can get anywhere by walking or taking the subway, you can find big luxury chains and little interesting mom-and-pop shops within a few blocks of each other, and you can be weird and no one cares.

You can sing full volume while walking to your audition, and no one will even turn around. You can practice your monologue on the subway and no one will be fazed. It's a city filled with interesting people who have learned to be fine with the eccentricities of its population. The flip side of that is that it's a good place to find your inner strength; you need a strong dose of independence and self-confidence to navigate this city.

FRIENDSHIPS

While you will make some friends in Broadway shows, it's not the same chummy atmosphere as you'll find on tour or in regional theatre. People come in and out, and for the most part, it's a job—they show up for performances and go home afterward. So if you're interested in theatre for the social aspects, you have the right personality for touring, which provides for some really cool bonding experiences.

Missed Holidays

Assuming your friends and family don't all live in New York City, you'll be away from them most of the time. Now let's say you get an invitation to one of your best friends' weddings. Can you go?

Maybe. It depends on who can cover you that day . . . or perhaps who *you* cover in the show. While I was working as a standby for Glinda, the full-time performer had already put in for a personal day, and the understudy had plans to take her family to Disney World. There was no one else in the building ready to play that role, so I had to turn down a family wedding. It was hard, but the reality is that this is a business, and the show must go on.

That's how it is with time off—according to Equity

contracts, you do get a certain amount of vacation time and personal days, but that doesn't mean you get to take them whenever you want. It's often a first-come-first-served approach with the stage manager and company manager, or based on how many covers will be in the building on that given day. You put in for the days you want and then hope you get approved. If not, then you're out of luck. But that's okay! You're performing on Broadway!

What can be even harder are the main holidays—almost everyone else is with their families on Christmas, but when you're on Broadway, you don't get the day off; you typically have *extra* shows. You might work two performances instead of one that day. Or instead of the typical eight shows a week, you might have nine, and you will definitely be working on Christmas Eve or Christmas Day. Remember that tourists love to experience the magic of New York at Christmas, and part of that magic is seeing a Broadway show during their Christmas trip.

After a while, you start realizing, *Hey, this is work,* and that is another example of where the *it's a job* aspect comes into play.

Don't get me wrong: It's still awesome work and a dream come true. It's an amazing way to make a living, and I'm so grateful that it's the career I get to have. But it is work. It's not the same as that fun weekend with friends performing in your high school musical. It's a big commitment full of sacrifices. If you don't love it down to your bones, it will take everything you have.

If you're lucky, you have understanding friends and family and find ways to make it work. When family friend and writer G. Tom Ward came to see *Wicked,* he was amazed by what we pulled off; it was my father's birthday and it was a Saturday, which meant I had two shows to do that day, with about four hours in between. After the matinée, I had to quickly change out of my costume and into my regular clothes and make it out quickly to the Azalea, a restaurant nearby where my mom and I had planned a surprise party for my dad—and most of the cast and crew were secretly headed there as well.

I had to account for the fact that there would be, as always, audience members waiting by the exit for autographs and pictures, which is always a delight. I built that time cushion into the start time of the party.

"For most people, setting up and hosting a surprise party would constitute a full day, but you fit it in between Broadway shows," Tom said in amazement.

Uncertainty

You never know when a show is going to end, so while you're on Broadway, you're still auditioning for other stuff. Sometimes you're really rolling the dice to leave one show for another, too.

During our *Wicked* run, several of us auditioned for *Titanic*, a revival coming to Broadway. Some got called back; some didn't. We were all talking about it and were so excited for our friend Kathryn when she received an offer to join the cast. She gave her notice and left our show and set out to rehearse for the next big opening . . . and it never happened. There wasn't enough money, and the show never made it to opening day. Just like that, she was unemployed again. That is a huge reality in this industry.

Even long-running shows end. They all do, eventually. And sometimes you'll have an idea that a show isn't doing well, while others are total surprises. Everyone in the cast can feel great about a new show and expect it's going to be huge and win Tonys, but if no one is buying tickets, it's gone just like that. *Poof.*

That's what happened to my friend Donna Vivino when she was starring in *Merrily We Roll Along* with Wayne Brady and Aaron Lazar at the Wallis in Beverly Hills, for which she was nominated for an Ovation Award. It was a short, sold-out run with Tony-nominated director Michael Arden, and expectations were high that it would transfer to Broadway.

But Wayne Brady was sick and didn't appear on opening night, and the press opening was postponed. When the reviews came in, they were not enthusiastic. While most praised the performances, they pointed to a problematic script and staging problems that one critic said made the show "difficult to fully embrace." It never went any further.

So you can't keep all your eggs in one basket. And if you figure that once you have Broadway experience, it'll be easy to pick up another Broadway show, well . . . wrong. You start over from scratch every time, unless the casting people happen to know and like you and you fit exactly the type they're looking for. Just because I have Broadway and national tour credits on my résumé doesn't mean that I can get seen for everything I want. Even after playing Glinda, I couldn't get seen for certain roles and auditions, which stunned me at first.

"I can't believe I can't get seen," I said once to my vocal coach, a woman who knows *everybody.*

"I want to tell you I can't believe it either, but this industry is flooded," she said.

It's a business where you're constantly proving yourself, constantly auditioning and trying to get your foot in the door. Training, training, training.

Given all that, you might be wondering at this point, *Okay, aside from Broadway, how else can I make a living doing what I love?* So glad you asked, because that's what we're about to discuss!

3

Your Options
as a Performer

If you are talented and you love performing—really, really love it and can't picture yourself doing anything else with your life and feel like your soul will die without it (because that's the only reason to follow this crazy career path)— then you can find a way to make a living in this field. It may just be in a different way from what you'd ever imagined before, because very little of performing is actually about fame and fortune, but there are nooks and crannies for performers in all kinds of places. Luckily, Broadway is just one street in one city, and there are tons of other ways to do this as a career. It really depends on your strengths, personality, and goals—you can carve out your own path, and it can change significantly as you go along and as your life changes.

When I set out to make acting my career, all I ever pictured was Broadway. Forever. I thought they'd have to wheel me offstage. But after more than ten years there, mostly back and forth between doing *Wicked* on tour and on Broadway, I had a defining moment that changed me.

It really started several months earlier, when I was walking down the street and ran into a theatre friend.

"How are you doing?" I asked.

"Annie!" she said. "I'm doing *Annie!"*

It struck me as so strange. I hadn't asked her *what* she was doing; I'd asked her *how* she was doing. But the thing is, performing is a career that will define your whole self if you let it. You lose your identity outside of your résumé if you're not careful to protect it.

Of course it's exciting to be cast in a big show, and it should make you feel good about yourself. After all, you had to beat out a whole lot of people to get there, which feels like a true validation of you and your talent. But it can't be your whole identity. It just can't. This business is far too fickle to attach that much weight to it. If you start buying into the hype that your worth is directly proportional to the size of your most recent role, then you're setting yourself up for clinical depression on a regular basis.

The problem, too, is how often fellow actors reinforce this. I have plenty of good friends who don't do this, but you will encounter many actors who judge you based on your current role. They'll smile and act effusive, but they're sizing you up and measuring themselves in comparison. It can be pretty gross—like the time when I was just getting back from tour and headed to the Gershwin Theatre to play Glinda again. I ran into an old castmate who noticed I was in the theatre district and said, "What are you doing here?"

There were apartment buildings nearby; I could have been walking home. But I knew what her question really meant; it meant "What show are you in?" and for once, I just didn't want to play the game.

"Just running some errands before work," I said.

"I'm doing *Cinderella!*"

There it was—at least she wasn't bothering to play modest. Of course I congratulated her.

"Where are you going again?" she asked me.

"Fifty-first Street," I said. It wasn't a lie—the Gershwin is on Fifty-first.

"Oh. Well, good luck to you, honey."

I knew from the piteous tone in her voice that she thought I was waitressing or something. And for the first time, I just didn't care. Had she known that I was actually going to a rehearsal . . . not just any rehearsal but a rehearsal to ride in the Glinda bubble, she would have been sufficiently impressed, and I would have had the validation of her congratulations. But the role had been such a defining part of my self-esteem for so long that I was starting to wonder who I was without it.

Between the national tour and Broadway, I had performed the role of Glinda about 1200 times and had been in the show as an ensemble member, Nessarose, and a swing close to 1500 times. It might be your two thousandth performance and your seventh show that week, or even your second show that day, but the audience is depending on you to perform it like it's opening night. You have to shine.

At the stage door following a performance, people often said things like, "Wow, you are so comfortable in that role!" "It's like you really are Glinda." "I guess you're not afraid of heights in the bubble!" "I'm sure you could do it in your sleep!"

I mean this in the most gracious way—yes, I am pretty confident in the role. Ha! I've performed "Popular" a thousand times, ridden in the bubble a thousand times, been strapped into the bubble dress a thousand times, been slapped by Elphaba a thousand times, and I have run down those famous steps into the castle at the end of the show in high heels and a huge ball gown without falling a thousand times. So yes. I *could* do it in my sleep. And I loved all those thousands of times and never took them for granted. Sure, there are days where you just don't feel like it, but you get over it and keep going because you know how lucky you are to have this cool job.

My favorite comment at the stage door was, "You must just *love* this!" And they were right again. I loved it all. But one night when someone said that to me, I thought, *I do love it, but maybe it's time for a change.* I realized I was ready to see what else was out there for me.

When you reach that place where you are ready for something new or different, it's not as simple as just leaving the show. It's your income. It's your routine. (And then you think, *Is that a good thing or a bad thing that I'm in a routine as an actor?*) What will happen when your contract is up? What will happen if you leave? How long until you find another show? (Which is why you continue to audition even while you are in a show.) If you don't find the joy in all of this . . . the ups and the downs, it will defeat you.

But as I learned, Broadway was not the final stop of my career. I hope and expect to be back there eventually, but there are so many exciting performing opportunities outside of Broadway, and I'm enjoying making my living as a performer in other ways. It's remarkable how many different avenues there are to do what you love *and* pay your bills. Here are some of the best options.

National and International Tours

Many shows go on the road; successful Broadway shows often have more than one touring company (and possibly international ones as well), and even shows that have never made it to Broadway can be successful traveling the country to other theatres, schools, and public spaces. National tours may be Equity or non-Equity. The first national tour coming off Broadway is almost always Equity, but subsequent tours may not be. The ensemble minimum pay rates for full production Equity tours are the same as the Broadway pay rates (about $1,900/week and up). In addition, actors on Equity tours are given a separate per diem check each week along with their weekly salary. The per diem payment varies depending on the type of contract.

Benefits

If you're looking for the tight-knit social aspects of theatre, tours are a great chance for this. You have lots of opportunity to bond with people because you're really living with them and depending on them; none of you are going home to your families or other roommates at the end of the day. I've made some of my closest friends on tour.

Some tours are national and long-running, while others are more limited, with just a few stops. Again, pay scale and professionalism vary. Often, people from the Broadway show wind up doing the national tours as well—and in cases like mine, people who had non-lead roles can step up here and prove themselves. Former understudies and standbys often take on title roles.

That was the case for three of us: I remember hanging out backstage with two of my friends, fantasizing about the roles we wanted to play. Christine was an understudy hoping to play Elphaba, Catherine was a swing hoping to play Nessarose, and I was a swing hoping to play Glinda. We were all working hard to show that we could do it. A year later, all three of us were in exactly those roles. The first time I was officially cast as Glinda was in that national tour, and it was everything I'd dreamed of. I remember the first time I went up in my bubble . . . I never wanted to come down. They were ready to take a required break, and I suggested that they just leave me there, please and thank you. I had been waiting for years to take a ride in that bubble, and no one was going to convince me to cut that ride short!

I never took a day off or missed a performance, even though I was entitled to. I had just wanted it so badly and fought for that role for so many years that I decided, *I'm never getting out of this bubble. I will be here every night. Holidays, vacations, whatever. Here I am.*

On tour, they provide you a per diem to cover your housing and food, and they're required to give you options for hotels or other group housing (usually at a good discounted rate). That's called *company housing*. But you can opt out of the company housing and decide on another place to stay.

On some occasions, I've chosen to room with another cast member at a hotel and save some of that stipend money. And sometimes the tour may pass through places where you have family and friends (or other castmates do), and you can crash at their houses and save the entire stipend. It's a great idea to save as much money as you can from tours because you have so few expenses, and the money you make can cover you during lean times. It's much harder to save money when you're living and working in New York.

And of course, you do get to travel. Depending on how long each stop on the tour lasts, you may have opportunities to go do touristy things, hang out with the locals, or do whatever else your heart desires. It's a good chance to see parts of the country you might not otherwise visit. There's a lot of variation on the length of each stop; with an Equity tour, you may be in the same city for six weeks, whereas with non-Equity, it could be two nights in one city, two nights in the next.

Tour audiences tend to be very enthusiastic. They're excited that Broadway-caliber talent is coming to their hometown!

Challenges

All that travel can be tiring. Sometimes you may just miss your own bed. You're living out of suitcases for an extended time—not all the comforts of home—and rarely getting to see your family and friends. It's a lifestyle that people can have trouble with, particularly if they're married.

Of course, if you don't bond with your castmates, the

experience is going to be a lot worse. While casts usually do get close on tour, the opposite can happen as well if anyone there is bringing in the *other* kind of drama.

It also means that you're out of the game for other auditions—while you're hanging out in middle America, New York is casting things without you. It's hard to plan ahead for your next job when you're on tour.

Regional Theatres

The professionalism and pay scale of regional theatres vary greatly, but the good ones can attract Broadway-caliber talent and pay a fair salary as well as providing housing and even sometimes a car. Theatres may be very large or tiny, intimate venues, and the shows can be anything from popular musicals to original one-acts.

Benefits

One of the best parts of regional theatre is that it allows for more creativity than Broadway does. It's not all about making a mass-audience-friendly show using a cookie-cutter formula that can be followed exactly the same way night after night. There is more of a chance for your own interpretation of a character, your own improvised add-ins, variations on blocking and vocal runs. Regional theatre is a safer place to experiment, and there are many more original shows. Even seasoned Broadway performers often like taking leaves to do some regional theatre just to feel creative again.

Some regional theatres are open year-round for in-house

shows, while others are seasonal (summer and/or school breaks). Some regional theatres, based on their union contract, can hire two Equity performers per show, some ten per show. Some are Equity-only.

Show runs are usually limited to a couple of months, whereas on Broadway, every show is produced with the hope that it'll go on for years and years. That can be a plus or minus depending on your perspective: Long runs can mean better job stability on Broadway, but regional theatres tend to use the same actors again and again in different shows, and so as long as you're happy there, you can find ongoing work.

There is often more audience interaction in a regional show because the theatres are smaller. You're not going to see things like free shoo-fly pies for all couples celebrating an anniversary or fifty-fifty raffles at intermission at a Broadway show, but that kind of thing can add to the charm of regional theatres.

Challenges

Living in a dorm sounds really fun in college. Beyond that . . . it's not always a lifestyle adults choose. And that's sometimes what regional theatres offer: dorm-style housing with shared bathrooms, and sometimes they put you up in a nice hotel.

When I am offered the chance to act in a regional theatre nowadays, I do take into consideration my surroundings and the toll of uprooting my life for a few months at a time. Do I want to pack up all my stuff and move to Kentucky for two months? You may see it as a fun adventure, or you may see it as a chore—it's all a matter of personal preference.

The pay can be good, or it can be . . . not good. Blue Gate Musicals, for example, will employ fifty non-Equity actors this year in tiny theatres in Pennsylvania, Ohio, and Indiana—for $300 per week. Keep in mind, of course, that housing and meal stipends are included (and internet and cable), but still, that's a salary of $15,600 a year with no health benefits. Yet you will find phenomenal talent among their actors. (On the flip side, larger regional theatres like the Muny, Music Theatre Wichita, and Maltz Jupiter Theatre that employ Equity actors pay significantly better, more in the range of $800 per week for Equity actors and at least $500 per week for non-Equity.)

Symphony Concerts

Performing with symphonies has become one of my favorite things to do. You need to be able to read music, and the singers they hire usually have a classical background. The symphony will send you your music, and not long after you'll show up on a Saturday morning for a run-through with the orchestra, followed by a concert that night and the next day—so you need to be a quick study! The set list might be something like "An Evening of Gershwin" or "Bernstein's Best" or "The Best of Broadway."

Most symphonies also have a pops concert built into their season, where a featured vocalist is brought in to perform with the orchestra. Payment varies based on the symphony and their budget. The symphony world primarily exists on the support of donors and ticket sales.

Benefits

It is definitely a privilege to perform with symphony orchestras. I *love* concert work because you're able to be yourself, speak to the audience, talk to the conductor, share the stage with a full orchestra . . . you're not playing a role or a character.

This type of work also keeps you on your toes. While doing a long show run, your voice and body can easily get accustomed to the same movements and the same vocal flexibility because the show doesn't change. It can't change. On the other hand, every symphony director creates a different concert program, so every symphony performance will have different material.

Time commitment is minimal; you're normally just there for a weekend.

In the concert world, you are hired for your sound. Your presence and appearance are obviously important, but not in the way that it is when you're being hired to play a role or character. It's not as subjective. If you have the voice they want, you're hired; they are not concerned with your height or hair color. Concerts are, most of the time, the world of "park and bark" (stand still and sing). It's about the voice and the orchestra.

Challenges

You have to do your own homework before arriving to the symphony. You receive your sheet music or score, and sometimes (not all the time) you're given a piano track of your part to assist with learning the music. Then you arrive and have typically no more than two rehearsals with the orchestra before your performance.

It's a difficult field to break in to, but don't be afraid to stick your foot in that door if you have the skills for it.

HEALTH HAZARDS OF TRAVEL

Sometimes conditions can be very challenging for performers who are traveling outside of their usual environments. This applies to people on tour as well as those traveling for a weekend or an extended run. You could wind up in a very dry environment that's not good for your voice, for instance, or a humid environment that triggers your migraines or allergies. You learn over time what precautions you need to take and adjustments you need to make for different conditions. Céline Dion, for example, has humidifiers built into the front of her stage in Las Vegas, so there's mist coming up right where she's standing to sing. For me, my worst reminder of how fragile our bodies can be happened right before a symphony concert.

Steamboat Springs, Colorado, is a well-known winter ski resort area with its top elevation reaching over ten thousand feet above sea level. When you're not accustomed to high altitudes, traveling to the mountains can mess with you pretty badly until your body adjusts. The most common form of altitude sickness can cause shortness of breath, dizziness, nausea, headaches, and muscle aches. (The more serious forms can cause fluid to build up in the lungs or brain and are life-threatening.) I'd had problems with the common form before, and I know now to have a doctor's prescription for oxygen and to ask for someone to set it up for me as soon as I land in a high-altitude area. This time, the company tried to do something good to accommodate me:

"What if we fly you to Denver and then put you on a bus from Denver up to the mountain so your body will have time to acclimate slowly? Then we'll have oxygen for you when you get here."

Great! I thought. I would drink plenty of liquids on the flight and bus, and it would be a nice, smooth transition.

Except it wasn't. The bus ride up the mountain was long and bumpy through a blizzard, and the motion sickness combined with the altitude sickness that arrived anyway just made it a double whammy. The bus dropped me off right at the concert hall for rehearsal, and I was supposed to walk in and perform immediately. The musicians were already there rehearsing, just waiting on my arrival.

As soon as I entered the room, the musicians began stomping their feet to welcome me—their form of applause—and I thanked them by throwing up all over the place upon arrival.

In front of everyone.

Then I did it again into a trash can that someone helpfully provided.

Then I had to rehearse. There was no other time; the whole orchestra was there just waiting for me to sing, and our show was the next day. I kept the trash can next to me on stage and got sick two more times during rehearsal.

It wasn't my prettiest moment. But this, too, is part of the glamorous life of a performer and I laugh about it now. There was no standby waiting in the wings for me. The show must go on!

Theme Parks

Theme parks regularly put on shows and hire performers, and you can find these casting calls in *Backstage* as well. Most of them hold auditions in New York at least twice a year and on location more frequently.

At Walt Disney World, for instance, there are currently thirteen stage shows running every day. The most popular ones run every hour or two throughout the day and into the early evening.

As of 2019, the minimum pay rate for their chorus members is $15.66/hour, and the minimum for chorus stepping-out and principals is $17.61/hour, with annual rate increases and built-in bonuses of $1,400 whenever a contract of at least twelve months is complete. People who perform more than one job get extra pay; dance captains, vocal captains, and fight/stunt captains get an extra $5.75/hour, swings get an extra 8 percent, and actors who do stunts get an extra $16.75/hour for their performances.

It's hardly limited to Disney, though. Even smaller theme parks usually hire at least a few performers. Dutch Wonderland in Lancaster, Pennsylvania, is geared toward younger kids and has three musical shows per day.

To give an idea of pay range for this type of work, pay for the most recently reported contracts at California's Great America was $600/week plus lodging and a shared rental car, $525/week minimum plus lodging at Hersheypark in Pennsylvania, and $552/week without lodging at Cedar Point in Ohio.

Benefits

Shows are almost always under an hour (about half an hour is more common) and long-running, so it can be a steady paycheck without a lot of memorization or difficult staging.

Some types of shows offer the chance to improvise and connect with the audience.

Drawbacks

You have to like kids to enjoy this kind of work, and at some venues you'll be performing outdoors regardless of weather.

Depending on the setup, you may be performing for people who are not sitting down and paying attention but are instead strolling through the park talking and ignoring you. At Knoebels Amusement Resort, performers are situated on a small stage right on the side of the main walkway, so it's rare for anyone to stay still to watch the whole show. It can be demoralizing to watch your audience leave while you're singing and dancing your heart out (on the other hand, the Disney musicals are inside buildings, and people normally do stay like in a normal theatre show).

It's also customary to do four to six shows per day spaced out with an hour or more in between—so there are a lot of pockets of downtime that aren't really long enough to go out and do anything.

Cruise Ships

Many musical theatre people wind up performing on cruise ships. It's a steady gig that allows you to show off in a variety of acts while traveling to beautiful places. There are, of course, some pretty big pros and cons.

Benefits

There are usually multiple opportunities for you to perform, and not just the same show every night. You might have several different main shows during the course of a cruise, plus possible solo and duet performances. For instance, cast members at Holland America learn five thirty-seven-minute shows and one twenty-five-minute show and are expected to participate in social dancing lessons. You probably won't get bored easily.

You also get passenger privileges, meaning that you can eat great food all day long, go swimming in the pool, see other acts, and so on. At least in some cases, you also get an alcohol budget. Bobby Logue, a former cruise ship veteran who now runs a regional theatre in Florida, says that he was given a stipend that he was expected to use to treat guests to drinks—just a little touch to make passengers feel special. But if he wanted to use that all on himself, there was no one watching over him—and the performers did spend plenty of nights getting tipsy in their cabins because they would run out of things to do. The performers and crew often get very close, considering the close quarters.

You'll usually get to leave the ship when it's at port, so you can go out and sightsee, go shopping, and do whatever you want to do. It may enable you to see parts of the world you wouldn't see otherwise. You'll also get to meet people from all over the world, and you're encouraged to socialize with the guests—so if you're a people person, that could be a lot of fun.

There's a friends-and-family discount on most cruises, so it's at least possible for your loved ones to visit you less expensively while you're at sea. And at least in some cases, the housekeeping crew keeps your room clean and your bed made for you, so it's like living in a luxury hotel full-time.

Another big benefit is the lack of expenses. They're not the highest-paying jobs in the industry (about $2,400–4,000/month), but it's respectable money and it's all yours—you don't have to spend any money on rent, utilities, food, and so on. You get to save every penny you make while you're on the ship.

Challenges

I know a performer who had an opposite experience of Bobby's—he did one stint on a cruise ship and would never go back again because the cast and crew didn't get along with one another. When you're stuck out at sea together for six months or more, things have the potential to turn disastrous. When the chemistry works out, it's great, but what do you do when you get all the way out there and realize you can't stand your new coworkers?

Even worse, what if you can't stand your *cabin-mate*? That's right—not all cruise lines will promise you a single cabin. Some offer single cabins only to the principals and give shared cabins to the rest of the cast.

The other related drawback is how isolating it is. You're really, really cut off from the outside world. I felt sad when I sometimes had to miss family events as a Broadway actress, but imagine being on a cruise ship—you literally have to miss everything that comes up. A friend is having a baby? Someone you love is in the hospital? You can't be there. Chances are that you may not even find out right away; even with the ubiquitous nature of cell phones and Wi-Fi, when you're out to sea or at remote locations, communications can drop out completely. And making phone calls from overseas can be prohibitively expensive. You're not going to be calling home every night or even every other night; those calls will be short and sporadic unless you want to blow your whole paycheck.

Also, whenever you're out on the ship, you're expected to represent the company—no coming out in sweatpants or jeans for breakfast. You have to be "on" and presentable all the time, and you must be friendly to the guests even when they may be obnoxious, drunk, or otherwise. You will likely have a curfew to get back to your cabin and a strict "no fraternizing with the guests or visiting their cabins" rule. You may also be expected to take on other duties while on the ship, usually in a social capacity, like running games.

There have been several health scares on cruise ships in recent years when nearly everyone on board came down with a bad virus—living in such close quarters does mean that germs spread easily, and a cruise can get disgusting fast if this happens!

Resorts

Most resorts hire performers of all types to entertain their guests on a freelance contract basis, but some popular resorts have in-house musical theatre entertainment. This is not usually a full-time position, but it can at least be regular part-time work and may include housing and meals.

Jennifer Kiesendahl auditioned in New York to join the cast at Pennsylvania's Woodloch Pines more than ten years ago and has seen her job evolve over the years as the resort's needs have changed. In the early years, it was more of a full-time job in partnership with another resort. Now they work two days per week, either two or three performances depending on whether or not it's a peak time.

They put on one themed show, and it runs for an entire year, with the new show debuting in time for New Year's Eve guests every year. The most recent show is a tribute to every decade of television, featuring theme songs and songs made famous on television shows. It's a cast of about ten to twelve people at a time, and contracts may run for six months or a year. There is a wide age range and not much turnover at this time.

All the performers have other jobs, most of them at the resort. "I've done social staff, cocktail serving, bartending,

I've worked in the marketing department, I've worked on the golf course . . . I've worn a lot of hats," Jennifer says. "I think the reality with most performance jobs is that you're going to be working other jobs as well, unless you get the big ticket or you're fine with eating tortillas all the time."

Jennifer says that she wasn't cut out for the competitiveness and businesslike nature of Broadway but that theatre was one of her formative experiences, and there were so many benefits to keeping it in her adult life. What she found at the resort was a perfect blend for her—and she ended up marrying the owner's son!

The cast rehearses for about six weekends because most of the performers have day jobs, and Jennifer says they come from all different backgrounds—some people have musical theatre degrees and lots of experience, while some have always been talented hobbyists. It's a tight-knit group, though it hasn't always been right for everyone. The resort is in the middle of nowhere—literally in the woods, in an area where you're not going to be surrounded by other theatre people (or much of anything else outside of the resort). So in addition to the audition, there's also an interview process to try to determine if candidates are prepared for the situation. For instance, there's no public transportation, so performers must have a car. Many have left after their six-month contract was up, but the cast now is mostly made up of longtime members.

"The benefits of a job like this are that you can broaden your perspective. You're performing, but you also have the ability to encounter people from all over every week. It's a job that allows for balance. You can perform *and*. So much of the performance lifestyle is all-consuming, but with this,

I'm able to be a full-time mother as well and teach yoga classes and try out a bunch of things. If you like it, then you don't ever want to leave."

Dinner Theatre

Dinner theatre is really just what it sounds like: attendees watch a show while they're eating dinner. These are often audience-participation type shows, with or without music. Murder mysteries and comedic shows are common in addition to well-known musicals and original acts. However, they've been on the decline in recent years, with many long-running dinner theatres closing their doors. Only the ones in touristy areas tend to do best.

Pirate's Dinner Adventure in Orlando, Florida, and Buena Park, California, has at least one show every night—but often two—and has been running for twenty years in the first location and ten years in the second. Dutch Apple Dinner Theatre in Lancaster, Pennsylvania, is about to celebrate its thirtieth anniversary. Toby's Dinner Theatre in Columbia, Maryland, has been running since 1979.

They share the same benefits and drawbacks of regional theatres, with the exception that many dinner theatre shows are longer runs, sometimes changing scripts once a year or less. And at some dinner theatres, the performers are also the waitstaff (or have the option of picking up shifts).

Companies with Equity contracts pay about $700/week plus housing and a per diem for out-of-town actors, and they can offer steady work. You can also factor in tips if the actors are also the servers.

Cabarets

People who've never been to them are sometimes confused about what *cabaret* means. It's a pretty wide definition nowadays, unlike its earlier days. The term started in clubs like Le Chat Noir and Moulin Rouge in France in the late 1800s, where it had erotic connotations and featured singers, showgirls, and comedy with elaborate costumes and sets. But in the United States today, a cabaret really just means a more intimate musical performance that breaks the fourth wall (where the singers look right at the audience and perform for them, rather than in traditional theatre where the premise is that the characters don't know there's an audience). Traditionally, patrons drink alcohol during the show. Sometimes there's burlesque and adult-themed material, but often not.

One of the great things about cabarets is that you can usually choose your own material (within the theme if there is one—sometimes it's jazz or show tunes or another genre, and sometimes it's just open to the singer's favorite songs across any genre that the intended audience will recognize). It requires less rehearsal time and less memorization of lines and blocking than a full-length musical, requires a minimal budget, and can be performed solo, as a duet, or with a bigger cast.

Benefits and Challenges

The positives and negatives of this one are mixed together: You'll have more interaction with the audience, and you're not playing a character. For some people, that's a lot of fun. For others, it's terrifying. I have friends who are great big hams on stage normally but who clench up when imagining just being themselves on stage; they'd much rather have a character to play.

With a cabaret, you're introducing your own songs, talking to the audience about why you chose them, telling stories from your life, or just chitchatting to engage them in what's meant to feel like a living room conversation. It's your patter, and it's a big part of what cabarets are. You should have an idea of what you're going to talk about between songs, but it's best if there's room for improv and real interactions with the audience. It's also customary for the songs to be story-based (have a plot, not just random catchy tunes).

Big theatres may host cabarets from time to time in between their regular shows, but they're more often in nightclubs and smaller venues.

Another great part of cabarets is that they're so easy to put together—you can do it yourself or grab a couple of your friends, start your own cabaret act, and pitch it to nightclubs and dinner theatres. It's a lot of fun!

Mounting Your Own Show

A friend of mine who played opposite me on the *Wicked* tour, Michael McCorry Rose, used to compare notes with me quite a bit. We developed a very close friendship on the road, and we were thrilled when we both had the offer to move to the Broadway company of *Wicked* together. Over the winter, when we had two shows a day, neither one of us wanted to go outside in between the shows—it was just too cold!—so we'd sit together and talk at the theatre instead. On one of those breaks, during a time when we were both frustrated about not getting seen for roles that we thought were perfect for us (yes, we were both auditioning during the week while doing *Wicked* at night, because *that's what you do*), we decided to take matters into our own hands: we wrote our own show and cast ourselves as the leads (and only characters)!

We called it *Cheek to Cheek: A Broadway Romance,* and we are still performing it now. It's full of new arrangements of classic love ballads and up-tempo songs from Broadway shows. We've sold our show to different theatres and cabaret venues across the country. Pay is determined based on what the space can offer—sometimes they pay us a flat fee, sometimes we rent the space from them and keep the proceeds. We also consider our travel expenses; if we have a show in Orlando, Florida, on a Friday night and that theatre is also covering our flight and hotel for the weekend, then we can take great advantage of that and play different venues on that Saturday night and Sunday matinée that might pay well enough but cannot fly us down or house us. These other venues are not ones that we could travel to Florida to do alone, so we schedule them when we can anchor them to a more prestigious venue.

Benefits

You can, of course, see the benefits of creating a show like this: You're self-employed, which means that you create the role you want and (within reason) the schedule you want, and you decide what to accept in terms of fees and conditions.

Challenges

But it also means using skills that may not come naturally to all actors—venues won't come looking for you, so you have to be your own promoter and businessperson. You're now in charge of booking the shows by making cold calls or sending emails, dealing with negotiating contracts and payment, publicizing the shows, and so on. It's more work than just showing up at the theatre and playing your part, and some of that was difficult for us.

In New York, where our show opened, it was hard to break through all the noise to actually sell tickets. We essentially rented a space to start, and then it was up to us to get bodies in those seats. We weren't getting paid a flat fee—we were getting paid a percentage of all ticket sales, so the audience size mattered *a lot.*

For a while, no one seemed interested, so we worked out a plan: we'd hand out postcards on the street while wearing our *Wicked* T-shirts so that people would know we were in the cast (and therefore probably good)! But it backfired on us a bit . . . people would come up to us to ask if we were selling tickets to *Wicked,* and as soon as we started to explain what we were actually doing, they would just walk away. Ouch. We ended up selling seats, but it was a lot of pavement-pounding. We were tempted to feel sorry for ourselves until we ran into one of Michael's actor friends, who was also handing out postcards to passersby—most of whom tried to avoid eye contact.

"Hey! What are you doing here?" he asked Michael.

Michael explained about our show and then asked what he was up to.

"I'm working for *Chicago*," he explained. Well . . . he was a ticket promoter for them, but he was hoping it would help him land an audition. Our hearts broke a little for him, and it gave us a dose of perspective that we could probably handle a little stint as salespeople if it meant we could continue working as actors.

Things became significantly better when we booked shows outside of New York and the theatres mostly handled ticket sales themselves. Then we could just show up and do what we did best. It was so empowering to mount our own show—like taking destiny into our own hands!

Now that you have an idea of your options, let's talk about some dos and don'ts of getting cast.

4

What *That Guy* Taught Me About Reputation

I kept running into this guy.

For a couple of years, he was like an irritating fixture at auditions. I have no idea if he was talented or what his background was; all I knew is that when people went in the room to sing, he would run up to the door and listen . . . and criticize.

"Who still sings *that* song? That's *so* overdone! Listen, people, nobody should sing that song."

"That note. Why would he go up on that note? That sounded terrible."

"She can*not* even walk in heels. Why is she wearing that ridiculous outfit?"

He was talking to all of us, just calling out his random

rude observations and occasionally his judgmental advice for the rest of us. I didn't appreciate it, and neither did the other performers. We'd give each other knowing glances and eye rolls as he went on his ugly rants.

Imagine my surprise when I ran into him on the other side of the table.

I had been in the national tour of *The Drowsy Chaperone* from 2007 to 2008 as an understudy for Janet and member of the ensemble. I was also the dance captain. The following year, after our tour closed, my director announced that there would be a non-Equity version of the tour as well, but he was unable to work on it due to other projects.

"You were my dance captain; I'd love to have you and an associate director put together the show if you're interested." I would be setting the original choreography for this tour.

"I would love to!" I gushed. It sounded like a terrific opportunity, and I didn't even realize how much of an education it would provide me. What it meant was that I would have a voice in the casting of the show, so for the first time, I would be one of those scary people I'd had to impress more than a hundred times before.

I sat behind a table with the show's director, musical director, and casting director, and we had copies of each performer's headshot and résumé in front of us during each audition. For the first round of auditions, we saw people from 9:00 a.m. to 6:00 p.m. for several days—a new performer every three minutes—and for the first time, I got to see the nonverbal method of communication some casting people use with one another: The casting director had put a piece of paper in the middle of the table with *Yes, No,* and *?* on it. When I wanted to communicate with the rest of the production crew about how I felt during an audition, all I had to do was nonchalantly point to one of those three things. This was used as a quick way to decide if someone fit the role or not. We could quickly glance across and know if we were in alignment or not and decide if we wanted to hear more or not.

Knowing what it's like to be in front of a casting team gave me a lot of empathy for the performers; I didn't want to cut anyone off. I wanted to get up from the table and hug each person before they sang, and I wanted to remind them to have fun and relax. I wanted to give everyone a chance—and then a second chance if they were blowing it because of nerves. But then *he* walked in the room. The obnoxious guy I'd seen at multiple auditions years ago.

It was like an instinct: I pointed to the *No* on the paper as soon as he approached the piano with his sheet music.

The casting director glanced over and called out, "Thank you. That's all we need."

I was so flabbergasted that I don't even remember how Obnoxious Guy reacted. We'd just dismissed him without even hearing him sing, and for a moment, I felt terrible.

"Why did you do that?" I asked.

"You want to give everyone a chance. If you said 'no,' I knew there had to be a good reason."

I considered it for a minute and realized that he was right; there *was* a good reason. I hadn't stolen his chance to be cast; he'd blown it all by himself by building a bad reputation and behaving like a total jerk time and time again. This business is flooded with talent, so why work with a talented jerk when you can easily find a talented class act? Be the class act.

Safeguard your reputation. In this business (and in any

business, for that matter) your reputation counts a *lot*. Even though there are so many people who want to be cast at high levels, you do tend to see the same people over and over. They're talented enough to have gotten their foot in the door, but the question is whether or not they can stay in the room.

Hollywood shows us that sometimes you can be a really big star and be really obnoxious. Movie stars get away with some famously terrible things on and off set—throwing drinks at people, going on screaming tirades, "Do you know who I am?" behavior, and so on if they can keep bringing in box office dollars. In the theatre world, that's a lot less prevalent. I'm not going to pretend that everyone working in theatre today is a lovely human being, but we have a lot less patience for bad behavior, and it's more of a family atmosphere. Whereas in movies, most of the time, you meet only the actors who are in your scenes and you work together for a few months, in theatre, you're more likely to be together for a year or more at a time and working more closely with the whole unit. Directors do find out who's causing problems within the cast, and if a director finds out you're making other people miserable, you won't get cast again in any of his or her future shows. It's so easy to find talented people who *aren't* jerks.

The story of Shonda Rhimes and Katherine Heigl is a cautionary tale; Heigl was a standout star on *Grey's Anatomy* and even won a Best Supporting Actress Emmy for the role in 2007, but in 2008, she wasn't satisfied with the story lines she was given and didn't submit herself for Emmy consideration, against Rhimes's wishes. When asked about it, she said to a reporter, "I did not feel that I was given the material this season to warrant an Emmy nomination."

That didn't go over well in the media or with Rhimes,

who didn't like the way that the actress had just insulted the show's writers. Although Heigl apologized, it stuck with Rhimes, who later described to Oprah the extensive background checks and vetting she did of future cast and crew members to make sure they would all jell with one another—even going so far as to later say that "there are no Heigls" in the *Scandal* cast. It had a strong negative impact on Heigl's career, and she wishes she had kept her mouth shut. It was a hard way to learn the lesson that complaints should never be aired in public.

My Governor's School teacher Alan Fischer says, "It can seem like the people with big egos get everything, but that only works for a little while, and then they come tumbling down and you never hear from them again. If you think you're God's gift, it'll tend to bite you at some point, because there's always going to be someone better than you. Always, always. And you never know when the person you stepped on two years ago is going to be the girlfriend, boyfriend, husband, wife of the director, producer, or agent. Karma comes around to get you."

Directors and producers have also mentioned being embarrassed by cast members' bad behavior on social media, particularly when they bad-mouth their shows or fellow cast members. Talk about shooting yourself in the foot! Even if you hate the script or the people you're working with, never say so publicly—first, because you need the show to have an audience, and second, because you don't know where those people will end up. You don't want to get shut out of an audition in the future because someone remembers that you said bad things about a show you were in before. Be someone others want to work with.

STAYING HUMBLE

• •

When the kids in Destination Broadway asked guest artist Jared Bradshaw about who was the nicest cast member in *Charlie and the Chocolate Factory*, he said, "The star, Christian Borle. He always takes time for everybody, and he knows everyone's names. He's been in this business a long time, but he doesn't act like he's a big star." That's how you want to be known.

"Don't flaunt your talent. You don't have to tell people how good you are. Just do your job and they'll know it," says Alan Fischer.

But enough about how to mess up your reputation. Now let's talk about how you can build your positive reputation as an actor:

- **Show up on time.** Rehearsals, performances, media appearances . . . being on time is just basic respect. Set your clock five minutes fast if you have a tendency to push it to the last second! Never be the last person into the theatre.

- **Be ready.** Know your lines, know your vocal parts, know your choreography. Be off-book before you're supposed to be off-book. Show up ready to work, without complaining about how tired you are. Be responsible with yourself— get enough sleep, eat right, and exercise so you'll be at your peak when it comes time to do your job.

- **Take notes well.** Be aware that you will get criticism in the form of "notes." Be humble in your reactions, and take these notes seriously. You can't keep making the same mistakes; there are too many people who want your job. Pay attention and fix any problems that come up. Even if you don't agree with the notes, take them, anyway; it's your job.

- **Avoid gossip.** Keep personal problems with others far away from the stage. When you start to hear someone complaining about a castmate, walk away. Don't get into taking sides in petty arguments. By the same token, of course, be willing to stand up for someone if something is seriously wrong.

- **Recognize other people's work.** We all know some people who try to suck up all the attention in the room by bragging about their accomplishments or telling stories that highlight how cool they are. Sometimes it's a defense mechanism, a way of saying, "I'm talented! I belong here!" Be aware that the theatre world isn't about being a star—it's about being a working actor. Even if you never get a lead role but you manage to support yourself through performing for many years, that's a huge accomplishment and potentially more impressive than someone who gets a couple of big parts but can't get steady work because no one wants to work with him or her again. Look for ways to recognize your fellow cast and crew members in positive ways, *especially* when the limelight is on you. Remember how many people quietly work behind the scenes while you and your fellow actors get all the applause. I always found it important to learn the names of the front-of-house staff, as well as the people working with us backstage, and engage them in conversation, too. They work hard to make us look good, and they deserve your kindness and attention.

- **Deal with your stuff.** Every one of us, unfortunately, will have difficult things happen. Deaths in the family, romantic breakups, landlord problems, friends who turn on you . . . whatever it is, it can be hard not to bring it with you to work. You arrive in a crummy mood and you're distracted, and you bring people down backstage. None of us are robots, nor can we be beacons of positivity all the time, but do your best. Find ways to deal with your problems (a therapist, support people, whatever you need) and try to set them aside the moment you walk through the theatre door.

- **Don't get everyone sick.** There will likely come a time when you need to perform even though you're under the weather, and you can't fully avoid everyone when you're going to be backstage and on stage with them—but do your best to isolate yourself. Sit by yourself with a book or your phone rather than joining in group conversations and coughing all over everyone!

- **Be generous with your time.** In the beginning, it feels like so much fun to sign autographs after a show. People want your autograph! You have fans! They want to take selfies with you! But after you've been at it for some time, a lot of actors are over it and they just want to go home, so they go out the "secret" door and skip out on the autograph line altogether. Resist this urge. Always remember that you have a job because those people showed up and paid for tickets . . . give them every reason to want to come back. Feeling personal connections makes for a better experience for audiences. When there are optional opportunities before or after performances (like meet and greets, backstage tours, cast parties, Q&A sessions), volunteer—and be willing to stay for more than just a few minutes. Some of the most famous, most successful Broadway stars are also the ones who will work the line until every fan has what they came for—people like Idina Menzel, Sally Field, and John Lithgow. I always made a point to do the same when I played Glinda; it helps the audience know that you appreciate them and want them to return! We wouldn't have a job without them.

- **Show that you're taking your craft seriously.** The best actors know that you never stop learning and growing. Stay humble enough to know that even after you've "made it," that doesn't mean you're done learning. Continue taking classes and workshops, continue practicing, and continue keeping your skills sharp.

- **Help others on the way up.** Do what you can to help your fellow actors. Don't be stingy with your contacts and recommendations. When you know of a good vocal coach, or a good agency, or a call that someone would be great for, share it—whether you expect it to come back to you or not. Put in a good word for people when you can, and help them with their projects. If you're leaving a show and you know someone who would be a great replacement, recommend them. (Sometimes casting directors are hesitant to take a chance on new people, but a referral from someone they trust can mean a lot. This is how Robert Anthony Jones made his Broadway debut—a friend of his had to leave *Finding Neverland* for a while and helped him get an audition as a replacement.) Remember there's enough room for everyone to thrive and be successful.

- **Don't be too good for anything.** I recently read a blog that amazed me; an actress who is still working on launching her career described how she walks out of auditions if they cut down to eight bars. As a professional, I can tell you that I've never walked out of an audition. If you're in a position where you're even *at* an open audition like that, then it's because you need work. You didn't get an appointment and you need a job.

Don't let ego stand in the way of your career. Never let it get to your head that you're above anyone else in this business; we're all out there with the same goal of making a living as performers, and we all need to do whatever it takes to get there. Stay humble. We don't need divas in this industry. Take the opportunity offered, even if you think it's beneath you. If they cut you to eight bars, sing the best eight bars you can, smile, and say, "Thank you." Meet people. Always be ready to grow.

You Never Know Who's Watching

A cruise line producer holds regular auditions in New York. When actor Bobby Logue came in to sing, he handed his material to the accompanist in the room and then sang his heart out to the people behind the table. He got the job. Only later did he find out that it had been a bit of a trick: the people behind the table weren't producers at all. The accompanist was.

The producer plays piano, so he figured it would be a much better way to judge people's true character if they didn't realize they had to impress him. He was paying attention to who said *please* and *thank you*. He was taking notice of who smiled and was polite when showing where they wanted the music cut. The people behind the table were just friends of his.

Now Bobby is the artistic director of BIG ARTS Strauss Theater on Sanibel Island, Florida, a not-for-profit non-Equity theatre working toward its Equity status. The majority of actors they hire are nonunion, but they can also hire two Equity performers per show on a guest artist contract. He holds auditions in New York once a season by open call and/or by submissions, and he has seen up to nine hundred people at a time within the three days he's normally in town. Unlike many directors, he makes it a point to see everyone who shows up, even if it means renting the space later or coming in earlier the next day before callbacks.

"I know what it's like to be on the other side, waiting around for six hours only to be told, 'Sorry, we don't have time. You can leave your headshot and résumé,'" he says.

"You feel like you're wasting your life, and I don't want to do that to anybody."

Of course he's looking for major talent, which is in no short supply. They have a healthy budget and provide condo housing and travel expenses, and they've been able to hire several Broadway actors or people coming off big tours. But just as important as talent, he explains, is personality. "I look for people who aren't crazy," he says with a laugh.

He learned a lesson from the cruise producer and incorporated his own version of it: Bobby hires monitors and proctors for the express purpose of having them take notes and report back to him about how people acted in the waiting room. The audition starts the minute the performers sign in, not the minute they start to dance or sing.

What's he looking for? How they treated other people. Whether they were being obnoxious about vocalizing, whether they were complaining or rolling their eyes about having to wait, whether they were bragging or being catty to try to psych out other people, whether they were rude to the monitor, whether they talked loudly on a cell phone while others were trying to concentrate . . . anything that would show signs of diva behavior or a lack of consideration for the actors around them.

Of course, he's also paying attention to how they act in front of him. He asks questions that are meant to seek out whether someone is even-keeled. One of his biggest turnoffs was an actor who wouldn't stop enthusiastically using the F-word during conversation. "No f——ing way! I love that f——ing show! I would be so f——ing excited to join the cast."

This is a job interview, Bobby was thinking. *I get that it's the theatre, but it's still a job interview!*

Another auditioner who'd been a great dancer insisted on singing right up against the table where Bobby and his associate were sitting. Even after they asked him to step back, he took a single step back and kept going. It was a red flag to them that this guy was aggressive and insisted on getting attention even against their directions. Signs of an ego—"I can do that. I can do anything"—can kill your odds.

"Even if you're the lead, you're still in an ensemble. There's a palpable heartbeat to a show, and the minute one person starts thinking it's all about them, it ruins the vibe of the cast. When you see a show, there's a big difference when you can tell the people on stage hate each other, or when they're working together and feeding each other energy. The minute it seems insincere, you lose the audience regardless of how talented individually the performers are."

He's keenly aware of the idea that the cast is going to have to live together and often share company cars—and that the experience can turn miserable fast if there are any cast members who think they're the best or who act obnoxiously. Conversely, people who are positive and caring can make the experience wonderful. So be that person!

5

Who Else Would You Be?
All About Auditions

Auditions can be maddening, nerve-racking, humbling things . . . but they can also be exciting when you get into good habits and find ways to tame your nerves and nail the part.

No one is completely at ease at an audition. If you didn't feel at least a little nervous, I'd say your heart wasn't in it enough. We're nervous because we care—we want more than anything to do well and impress the people we're auditioning for because this is what we love to do. If we didn't care so much, the nerves would go away, but so would the magic.

The good news is that you do get more control over this with experience. As your credits grow and you get some external validation of your talent, you should be more and more at ease that you've earned your place in the audition room, at least. And just the act of auditioning over and over can help it be less scary because you'll have a better idea of what to expect. But your goal should be to get a handle on them as quickly as possible because you won't be at your best when your nerves are high—your voice can get pinched and high-pitched, your hands may shake, your voice may shake, you may not be able to keep steady eye contact, you may forget your part, and so on. Part of doing your job is to train yourself to get in control so you can be at your best.

Learn to Focus

First, figure out where the nerves are coming from. Is it strictly about how much you care, or is it also about being underprepared? If you're not solid on your sides, your music, or your dance skills, that's understandably going to cause you to be nervous. It should also send you a strong message that you need to do a better job preparing in the future. Winging it doesn't work. If you're insecure about your songs, work with a vocal coach and make sure they're the right ones for you. If you're worried about picking up dance routines, take classes and keep working at it.

But assuming you are prepared, then there are two techniques I recommend for dealing with this:

- **Slow, diaphragmatic breathing:** Focusing on your breath is a great way to get grounded and to slow down a racing heart. You can do it wherever you are, and no one has to know you're doing anything. Focus on taking deep breaths that expand your belly instead of the shallow breaths that just expand your chest. Breathe in slowly through your nose and out through your mouth even slower. Count off mentally (*One Mississippi, two Mississippi, three Mississippi . . .*) and try to get a slow, steady rhythm going. Don't think about anything except your breathing. When other thoughts arise, just quietly dismiss them and keep your focus on your breathing.

This is a technique used in yoga, as well as in many acting exercises to get the oxygen flowing through your body and to help you get centered in your body so you feel more in control. Keep at it until you feel calm, and do it shortly before you get into the room. You can practice this at home by lying on the floor with a book on your abdomen; you want to see the book slowly rise and fall without having your chest significantly rise and fall with it.

- **Positive visualization:** There's good reason behind the mantra "If you can see it, you can achieve it." When you picture yourself successfully completing any sort of task, you form a blueprint in your mind. Olympic athletes will often tell you that they visualize their routines or events hundreds of times before the big day arrives, and it gives them not only a mental edge but even a physical edge because the movements become more automatic. When you get to an audition, after you've situated yourself and done some diaphragmatic breathing, close your eyes and picture yourself walking through the door into *the room,* smiling and saying, "Hi! My name is . . . ," to the creative team, having them greet you back and ask how you're doing.

Imagine them as friendly people who want you to succeed, and then see yourself taking a deep breath and going through your audition with confidence, nailing it. Hear yourself saying your lines, singing your song, doing your dance routine . . . whatever's coming up for you that day. Picture their faces smiling and nodding at you and telling you they loved it. See yourself walking out of that room with the knowledge that you just gave the best audition of your life—and that after you leave, the creative team is discussing how great you were.

Every time.

It can be challenging to put this into practice in a busy audition studio when you're surrounded by fellow actors who want to talk—especially when they're friends or acquaintances you haven't seen in a while—but if you spend your time chatting with the person next to you instead of getting yourself prepared and then you don't get a callback, you're going to be mad at yourself. It's okay to say, "Do you mind if we talk after the audition? I just need to get myself focused right now." Most people will understand. This is your career, and you need to make it your priority. Don't worry about seeming rude. You're just doing what you have to do to be at your best. It's time just for you. You may want to close your eyes or put on headphones to signal that you don't want to be disturbed. You should also open your book of music and read through it, even if you know it backward and forward. Just read the lyrics all the way through as a reminder.

The overall idea is to recast your nerves as excitement.

Check in with yourself and tell yourself that this is true:

I'm not nervous, I'm excited! It's okay if you don't fully believe it at first. Keep sending yourself that message. It's like "Fake it till you make it"—even *pretending* that you're not nervous can help you be less nervous. Talk yourself through what you know:

I am here because I belong here.

I am ready for this.

I'm prepared.

I'm right for this role.

This is what I love to do.

The creative team can't wait to see me.

I'm so excited to show them what I can do.

I'm going to nail this audition.

Pick any affirmations that feel right to you and keep saying them to yourself. No one can build your confidence the way you can. Work on consciously changing your thought patterns from negative (worry) to positive (excitement). When you catch yourself thinking negatively, just reframe the thought and say it to yourself again in a positive way. Talk to yourself the way you'd talk to a good friend.

When you're waiting around at an audition to sing or act, you also need to keep your voice warmed up—but how do you do that without being obnoxious to everyone around you? Hum! You can quietly hum and still keep your vocal cords ready to go. Make sure you're also drinking water or tea to stay lubricated.

THE FLOW OF OPEN CALLS

At an open call, most of the time, people are seen in the order they arrive. You'll likely be kept in a holding room while waiting for your turn, and often the casting director will ask people to come out in groups of ten or twenty. You still won't go into the audition room as a group, but you'll wait out in the hallway together as each person is called in one at a time, and then the casting director will go to the holding room for the next batch.

That hallway time is really "go time." That's when you need to concentrate on no one but yourself, just breathing and getting yourself centered and in the moment. Be prepared for the idea that you may not get seen at all during an open call; sometimes the creative team will call in a group of people and just point and say, "You, you, and you . . . ," and dismiss the others without seeing them at all, just based on appearance or résumé. That's called *typing* (as in, "these people are the right type"), and getting cut here is called *typing out*. Even though it may sound frustrating, it also prevents you from wasting time, and it leaves you understanding that the reason you didn't get the part had nothing to do with your talent.

Despite its drawbacks, at least early on, open calls may still be your best (or only) shot, so keep preparing and getting yourself out there despite knowing that there will be disappointments and that some dismissals will seem unfair.

Be Yourself

Aside from talent and a positive reputation, the other ingredient you need to be successful sounds clichéd, but I can't help it—it's really true: Be yourself.

When I say that, I mean walk into an audition as you, not as who you think you should be. Don't try to make an entrance in character; that doesn't work and is too transparent. Don't try to go for roles that aren't in your wheelhouse and where you don't fit most of the physical characteristics in the breakdown. In school and local plays, a director will often cast someone who doesn't look the part just because they're working with a limited number of actors who can audition and they can't be too picky—a high school senior can be cast as the wise grandfather because there are no grandfathers in high school, whereas in professional theatre, it would be a waste of time for him to go in for the role. Believe me when I tell you that if a call goes out saying that a director is looking for a redheaded twenty-five-year-old woman who plays the ukulele and can juggle five flaming pumpkins, there will be a line out the door of women who can pull that off.

You have to have both the look they want and the skills and vocal range they need. You should have a sense of what your type is and what kind of roles you're good at playing.

I had a hard time learning this lesson because in college, some of my professors were actually trying to change my persona. I'm a naturally bubbly, smiley, enthusiastic, girly-girl type. They saw that as fake and figured that, deep down, I must really be far edgier and more depressed . . . so they kept trying to get me to act out these edgier parts.

"You will never be a true actress until you find the darkness within yourself," one of them said.

So I tried. Of course I've lived good and bad experiences like everyone else, but searching for "the darkness" didn't feel natural for me. None of the material felt good. They weren't the types of roles that I understood or felt right playing, yet they were the ones my college professors wanted to see—so they'd say things like, "Good! You're finally being the real you!" and I would think, *No, I'm not . . . this isn't the real me at all.*

I left school very confused about who I was supposed to be at auditions. I figured that, to please professionals, I should tone down my real personality and try to be darker and less happy. I didn't want anyone to think that I was a phony . . . but the irony is that I was *being* a phony just so no one would think of me that way!

After some time (and lots of rejections), I realized I couldn't let a couple of professors who never really understood me dictate how I would run my career. I had to be me. And I quickly learned that casting directors responded to me so much better when I was being genuine. Finally, I got callbacks. My agent started getting calls to say, "We remember seeing Tiffany audition for another show of ours, but it wasn't quite the right part for her. Would she like to be seen for this new one?"

That's half the business right there; the odds are against you every time you audition for anything, but the more you get yourself out there, the more directors and producers get to know you and figure out where to place you. They can't place you properly if they don't see who you are. It's useless trying to become something you're not for an audition; walk in as you. Bring your own strengths to your characters.

During auditions when I was helping to cast *The Drowsy Chaperone,* I was thrilled to finally get to put this into practice. A woman had a little mishap closing the door behind her when she walked in, and she made a funny comment about it, smiled widely, and made us laugh. Then, when she was reading her sides—which was a comedic scene—her natural humor and personality vanished. She was trying too hard. The reading just wasn't working.

We had lots of other people to see that day, and we could just have easily said, "Thank you. Next," but something told me that this woman deserved a second shot. So I said, "You were really funny when you walked in this room. I want you to take a moment, relax, and then I want you to read it again. This time, I want you to just be yourself and read it honestly."

We ended up hiring her for one of the roles.

I wish someone had done that for me! I thought. There aren't a lot of second chances during auditions just because of timing, which is why it's important to get focused and get it right the first time. Remove the whole word *try* from your mentality. Don't *try* to be anything. Just be a confident version of yourself. Walk into that room with the knowledge that the people on the other side of that table really *do* like you and really *do* want you to succeed. Even if they look cold, they want nothing more than for you to nail your audition so they can cast you in the role you want. Repeat that to yourself over and over. Go in there with the belief that they already like you and that they're rooting for you. Because they are.

That doesn't mean you'll be right for every role, or that

even if you are right for it that there aren't ten other people who are just a little bit *more* right for it, but it does mean that you'll build up your reputation. Every time you're seen is a chance not only to be cast in that particular show but to get thought of next time there's a part even more suited to you—and that's true of theatre, film, and television.

Kevin Williamson, creator of *The Vampire Diaries,* says he regularly works this way.

"There's a lot of actors out there that I audition, and they're not right for the role, but they 'pop,' so I keep bringing them back because I know that eventually they're going to walk into the room and be perfect for the part," he said in an interview with *Backstage.* That was the case with Claire Holt, who originally tested for the pilot of *The Secret Circle* but was cast instead on his next show, *The Vampire Diaries,* in a role that she's still playing almost seven years later in its spinoff show, *The Originals.*

Theatrical director Schele Williams agrees, saying that she's often had situations where someone's not quite right for the show or she's precast a role that the auditioner is trying out for. "I don't think you can ever teach someone how to be rejected because it's never a good feeling . . . but I do tell students I coach that if you go into the room and you do your best work, and you have a good audition, whether you get the job or not, they will remember you," she said on the PBS show *Broadway or Bust.* "You can walk away knowing, 'It's out of my hands.'"

In this business, *no* doesn't mean "forever." It means "not this part, not right now," but when you go in with a good attitude and a great audition, it can very well mean something even better will come your way.

YOU CAN'T JUST BE OKAY; YOU HAVE TO BE GREAT

As much as I emphasize that you need to get yourself out there and do a lot of auditions, you also have to be selective about picking calls where you can shine. When a role calls for an alto and you're really a soprano, or where it's a tap call and you took a couple of classes once upon a time, don't go. When you have to learn a song that doesn't really suit your voice, or when you're pushing it to fake an accent you don't really have down, don't go. When you're a little under the weather or exhausted and you know your voice isn't at its best, don't go meet a casting director for the first time (if it's a callback and you have to, of course go and do as well as you can).

No one hires actors who are just *okay* at the audition, and it can harm your chances of getting future appointments. If a casting director sees you audition for *Waitress* and you're good but not great, then when you submit your headshot and résumé for another show they're casting, you might not get an appointment because they'll remember that you weren't great before. Stick to auditions where you can be great.

The Role of the Casting Director

My friend Cesar Rocha is a longtime casting director for Telsey + Company, where he works on theatre, film, and television projects. He explains that his role is like a personal shopper for the director. He doesn't make final casting decisions; his job is to get the right people in front of the show's production team. To do that, he needs to see lots and lots of people. He might see them first apart from the show's team, and that's called a *prescreen.* Or he might be there in the room with the show's team, helping to fill in details about what he knows about the performers.

His job is to make sure that no one's time is wasted. He'll book the audition space and set up the dates and times, and then he'll send out notices to agents telling exactly what he's looking for and what he wants to see. He will winnow out people who are clearly not right for the show or clearly not ready for professional work, and he'll book appointments with the ones he thinks are the best bets. He'll keep things moving along during auditions and will take notes about whoever he thinks is promising, whether for this show or another.

For instance, he'll mark up a résumé when he spots something interesting on it. Let's say a woman is nailing her vocal audition, but she's not their top pick for the part for one reason or another. But on her résumé, he sees that she's played Peggy Sawyer in *42nd Street. Wait a minute,* he thinks. *That means she has to be a really great tap dancer, because that's an intense tap dancing role.* So he circles that on her résumé so he'll remember it, and he keeps her headshot and résumé on file so that the next time he needs a tap dancer who can sing her face off, he knows who to call in. She may not even get a callback for the current role, though, so she doesn't even realize how much she's impressed Cesar, but he's just added her to his talent files, which is just what he wants—his goal is to get to know as many talented performers as possible so he has people in mind anytime a director calls him with a specific request.

Once you get to know him, he's also your advocate in the room when things don't go perfectly. Let's say you're a little under the weather at a callback; he's the one you'd tell beforehand so that later if there's a question about how you did, he can explain: "I've seen him audition before and nail that song, but he's just getting over being sick today. I think he deserves another shot." Or: "She's not a great auditioner—she gets nervous—but I've cast her before in two shows and she was fantastic." There's also a chance that he can get you an appointment a few days away so you have a chance to recover first.

(The advice is different when it's a first audition and you've never met him before. He says that telling him you're sick in that case only harms his impression of you. He has no way to judge if you're any better when you're well, and you shouldn't risk damaging your voice. There will be other auditions.)

Because casting directors get to know so many performers, directors and producers do turn to them for advice, which can range from wanting to know if a person is vocally capable of carrying a big show to asking if the person is pleasant to work with. That's another reason you want to be careful about your reputation. If you're the one who throws a fit when told that auditions are ending at 5:00 and you won't be seen, then you may lose an advocate at the next audition. You want to be known for good reasons, not stand out for being a complainer, an egomaniac, or unreliable.

RUNNING LATE

Of course you shouldn't be late—it can result in missed opportunities or just leave people with bad impressions of you—but we all have unforeseeable circumstances every now and then, and what's important is to communicate as early as possible. If you have an agent, call the minute you know you're running late. The agent should be able to text the casting director in the room to ask if you can be seen a little later or if you can reschedule.

It's Not About Them

I don't need to remind you how competitive a field this is. You know what it feels like to audition for something and check out the other people waiting for their turn, wondering if they're better than you are, if they're what the creative team is looking for. Actors walk into the room; actors walk out of the room. It's almost instinctual to check out their faces and body language to try to figure out how well they did (or how well they *think* they did), but it's impossible to guess accurately. It's also impossible to guess whose look the creative team is going to like or not like.

It's tempting to listen in on other people's auditions and use them as a barometer for your own. *Wait, that inflection she just used on that line . . . I don't say it like that. Should I? Is that how it's meant to be read? Should I put more energy on that word? Maybe I'm wrong about what the scene is about.*

Or, *He chose a really big song. Maybe I should switch my song to something in my book that's more belty.*

Or even, *I probably should have worn more makeup and curled my hair like that.*

Keep in mind that people are thinking the same thing about you.

And when you hear that someone is being asked to sing more, or that someone is staying in the room for a long time, torture! You think, *That's it. This person is probably just what they're looking for and now the role is going to be taken.*

Opt out.

There are way too many opportunities in this field to compare yourself to others and to second-guess your own choices and your own talent. When you're not really grounded and focused on your own audition while you're waiting your turn, it can really throw you off your game to snoop on others. Sometimes it's impossible to ignore altogether—you will hear some music through the door, for instance, but do your best to just block it out and stay in your own mind space. This time isn't about them. It's about getting yourself ready to show up in that room and be at your personal best, which has nothing to do with what inflections anyone else used. Don't try to make last-minute adjustments based on reactions to others. Do what you came there to do.

Being self-centered is normally not a positive adjective, but in an audition? It really is. Get centered on yourself. You ever look at a good photograph where the subject is in razor-sharp focus and everything around the subject is blurred, just there to give some color and shape? That's you at an audition. You're razor-sharp. Everything around you is background fuzz.

It's Okay to Say No

Let's say your agent calls you with an opportunity to audition for a new show. You read the sides, and for whatever reason, you don't like it. Maybe the material just sounds boring, maybe it's not your kind of part, maybe you feel uncomfortable about something in the script. Or maybe you're just exhausted and need a break.

It took me a long time to learn that it was okay to say no.

I thought that if I didn't agree to every audition that my agency scored for me, they would be mad at me and would stop sending me out for work. That isn't true. Of course they want you to be agreeable, but that doesn't mean you have to do every audition that comes your way. You are allowed to say no when you have a reason to, and it won't change how well they'll represent you in the future (unless, of course, you asked them to set you up with this audition and *then* you turned it down!). They're on your team; they want you to be happy.

I recently turned down a touring opportunity that came in through my agent because I'm just not up for months of traveling right now. You don't need to worry that your agency is going to drop you unless you're being unreasonable and turning down everything. In cases like mine, it was good to have that discussion with my agent because it let him know that he shouldn't send me out for tours for now. It's smart to have talks with your agent from time to time to make sure your goals match up; they need to know if they're not finding the right work for you, because that's a waste of both of your time.

For open calls, too, don't feel obligated to go out for every one of them if you don't like the material.

The exception to this is when you have no other work coming in and you just need a job. At that point, you don't get to be picky. We all need to pay our bills; if that means you take on a cheesy voiceover role, then that's what you do. It could be a lot worse!

Cultivate an Attitude of Gratitude

You already know going into this that acting isn't an easy way to make a living—or even to have as a hobby! There are lots and lots of rejections, show closings, lost opportunities, bad reviews . . . it can be disheartening and very emotionally challenging to keep picking yourself up and doing it all over again. Many people get stuck on complaining about the rough sides of this business, but it can be life-changing to focus on gratitude instead.

Of all the jobs you could have, you get to have one where you entertain people—you give them an escape from their troubles and routines. You get to do something you love that's exciting and interesting, and at the end, people clap for you. You get to meet fun people on the same path as yours. People in the audience get so excited to watch you do your job that they wait around afterward just for the chance to meet you and tell you how great you were. That doesn't happen when you're a postal worker or a sales representative!

Every night I was in the bubble, I always said, "Thank you, God, for putting me on this stage and giving me this opportunity. I'm so excited to be doing this." Even the five hundredth performance.

The energy you bring to the room can be contagious—both positive and negative. (Have you ever been near someone who just brings the whole mood down?) Carry good energy with you to your auditions, rehearsals, and performances, and people will be drawn to you. Even in the down times when you're looking for your next role, focus on being glad that you get to do this and feeling grateful for the next opportunity and the next. Stay in practice, keep learning, and try to remember how lucky you are to have the talent and drive to succeed.

6

Preparing for an Audition or Performance

A friend of mine likes to say, "Auditioning is the job. Performing is the vacation." After reflecting on it, I realized he was exactly right; the true grind of being a working actor is all the stuff leading up to getting cast. So often, we think that talent alone is going to be what sells us, but I can tell you from my work casting a show that some of the people with the best résumés—the ones who "should" have been shoo-ins based on how talented they had to be to play those roles—had some of the least impressive auditions. They got overconfident, I think, and didn't do the work of preparing for their audition.

Aside from submitting a tape (which we'll get into later), there are two ways you may audition for a professional show:

You might show up for an open call or Equity call, or you might get an appointment—usually through an agent or manager. Getting the appointment is always preferable for a few reasons, but one of them is that you'll get the material in advance. The lines you're expected to read and the instructions about what's going on in the scene(s) are called *sides*. You'll get your sides either from your representative or from someone in casting, often by email.

Of course you're expected to learn the sides. That should go without saying, and yet some people show up having only glanced at the lines a few times, and it shows—it looks like the performer doesn't really know what's going on and doesn't have the timing or the emotions down. A *cold read* is when you don't get the material in advance and you're just expected to show up and read whatever is put into your hands . . . it's great if you have the skill to pull that off well, but lots of people don't, and that's okay, too. Cold reading is the norm when you're auditioning for commercials, but in theatre, it's a lot more important to be able to learn a part and come in prepared.

Ask any casting director and you'll almost always hear that their biggest pet peeve is when performers aren't prepared.

"Especially in these open-call scenarios, where we're sitting in rooms auditioning hundreds of people in one day, and it feels like they just walked down the hallway and saw, 'Oh, look! Someone's holding an audition. I'll just step in and waste two minutes of their time.' I get that feeling a lot as a casting director," Benton Whitley of Stewart/Whitley casting said to *Backstage*.

So what's expected of you when you get your sides? I'm so glad you asked!

Have It Mostly Memorized

The goal should be to get the material memorized. It's a lot easier to focus on making eye contact with your reader and getting into the part when you have it down solidly. But that's not always practical, especially when you're expected to read more than one scene and you haven't had a lot of time to prepare. (You'll usually have just a few days' advance warning before your audition and almost never more than about ten days—and you may be preparing for several auditions at once, or also performing in another show while you're auditioning.)

Still, get it down as best you can just by repeating it and repeating it. But here's where it may sound funny: Even if you do have it memorized, keep the sides in your hand, anyway. Casting directors get frustrated when they see people empty-handed because they know it can mess up the read. People who think they have the material memorized may get thrown off by nerves, a new atmosphere, or a reader who reads differently from what the performer imagined, and then suddenly there's a long pause and an "Oops . . . line?" that takes away from the moment.

So keep it in your hands but refer to it as little as possible. The idea is to just have it there to guide you in case you have those moments of forgetfulness.

Why Are You There?

Beyond learning the lines, though, you also need to understand your character's motivation in the scenes. What happened before this scene? Why is your character happy/sad/distrustful/nervous/whatever emotion? Where did the character come from before this, and what has led to this point in the script?

It's a good idea to take an extra few seconds to orient yourself once you're in the room. Even though I've stressed that everyone in casting is pressed for time, that doesn't mean they want everyone to rush through their auditions. They really do want each performer to do their best work, so they understand if you need fifteen extra seconds to look around the room and place things in your imagination.

Very rarely is a character just standing in the middle of an empty room and talking to the audience. Pay attention to any cues you have about where your character is and what else and who else is around. If it's not specified, make it up. Get on that stage or in that room and place the bed, or the desk, or the crowd of people where you think they belong. It will help your focus and your eye movements in the performance. When an actor doesn't have a set in mind, he or she tends to look around aimlessly or just stare at the production team, which doesn't come across well. The people behind the table are not in your scene (unless you're breaking the fourth wall), so don't look at them. You want to be as believably swept up in the scene as possible.

When you have a scene partner, someone will be reading the lines opposite yours. The person will usually be sitting in a chair, but sometimes the director will have them get up next to you, which is always better. Either way, don't be afraid to fully use your scene partner. It's okay to walk up to them, touch them on the shoulder, play off them, and so on.

QUESTIONS TO ASK YOURSELF

Here are some questions to think through, both as you're learning your lines and while you're orienting yourself before an audition:

- **What does my character want?**

- **How does he or she plan to get it?**

- **What does the other person (or people) in the scene want?**

- **How does my character feel about the other person or people?**

- **What is my character thinking about and feeling in this scene?**

- **Where is my character coming from before entering this scene?**

Know the Show

When you're auditioning for a known show—something that's already running or has run before, see it! Do what you can to either catch a performance before your audition or at least watch a movie version or whatever clips you can find online. If it's based on a book, read the book.

See if you can get your hands on the whole script and give it a quick read. It may lend depth to your performance, and it can help you understand a scene better when you can flesh out your character in a more three-dimensional way.

Know the Players

In addition to knowing the show, it's also smart to know who you're auditioning for. Who's producing the show? Who's directing? Who's the playwright and composer? Who's the musical director? Who's the choreographer? What have they all done before? It shows respect for your industry when you take the time to get to know the players in it and what they look for.

One complaint I've heard from casting directors is that younger performers fresh out of school often don't know the history of the industry. They know all about the current-running Broadway shows and maybe the ones from ten years ago but not the older shows that inspired the newer ones. They focus only on what's happening on stage and their fellow performers rather than on the whole industry that got them this opportunity. If you're serious about being in this business, it's a great idea to follow the awards shows, read the industry publications, follow industry pros on social media, and learn about what people are proud of and what they're working on. Don't *just* focus on the new contemporary composers who are currently writing on Broadway; take the time to learn about the classics like Bernstein, Rodgers and Hammerstein, Lerner and Loewe, Irving Berlin, and Cole Porter. On an audition breakdown, you will often see "Please sing something in the style of Lerner and Loewe." You need to know what that means.

When you're auditioning for a new show and you can't get your hands on a full script, it can be helpful to get a better picture of someone's body of work so you can make educated guesses. Characters in Rodgers and Hammerstein musicals are very different stylistically (speech patterns, body language) from characters in Stephen Schwartz musicals. And when you get to know directors, you can start to see patterns in who they cast. Do they like subtlety in acting, sort of like screen acting on stage? Or do they cast people who are more like caricatures? Can you see any similarities in the styles of actors they hire? This, of course, often depends on the style of the show.

Even though I strongly believe in entering an audition as yourself, that doesn't mean you can't make choices that fit in with a director's known likes and dislikes. If I know a director likes understated actors, then I'm not going to show up in a frilly purple dress. I'm not going to arrive looking like I'm in *costume.*

A lot of this just comes with experience and the time it takes getting to know different directors, and also knowing what's right for the style of the show; don't make yourself crazy in the beginning trying to second-guess it all. Just do your best to stay in the know by studying the industry and it will get easier.

Training

Even as a working actor, I've hired a coach from time to time to work with me on audition material, and I've taken workshops focused on auditioning. Auditioning really is a skill of its own; some people are great at auditioning but less able to sustain their energy during performances, whereas other people get really wound up and nervous about auditions in front of a small group of pros but are comfortable in front of a general audience.

A lot of it is about mind-set—walking in with confidence and being as prepared as you can be. It's about wanting it badly enough but not coming across as desperate. It's a skill you can practice and hone just like any other skill, like learning to play an instrument or practicing a sport. You have to put in the hours and learn from people who do this for a living—and never get "too big" to continue training. Even when you're highly experienced, there's always more to learn. It can feel so intimidating at first to stand in front of a table full of casting professionals, but stick with it long enough and the confidence will become more genuine.

Your Singing Audition

When you're starting out, you will need to put together your "book," which means your sheet music for several songs that will fit different styles of music and different character types. It's smart to work with a vocal coach to pick out not only the songs that best represent you but to also have eight-bar, sixteen-bar, and thirty-two-bar cuts and full songs ready to go. If you're working on a cut, by no means do you have to start at the beginning of a song. Pick the part of the song that shows off your voice the best and tells a story. Usually people go to the end of the song and work their way back. You don't want to leave it on a random "middle spot" that isn't memorable. And if you go eighteen bars instead of sixteen, no one's actually counting. It's just an approximation of how much time you have. But don't push it further than that.

Almost all open calls will require sixteen or thirty-two bars, and you must bring your sheet music with you for the accompanist, marked where you're going to begin and end. No staples. The sheets should be printed double-sided or placed front-to-back in sheet protectors in a three-ring binder to minimize how many times the accompanist will have to flip pages. Try not to pick something with lots of crazy chord changes or a difficult arrangement because you don't want to worry that an accompanist looking at it for the first time will have trouble playing it.

Given the choice between singing something you know really well or trying something new just a few days before an audition, always go with what you know. You're much less likely to be undone by nerves, and you will perform it with great confidence.

Despite that I'm telling you to prepare cuts, also be ready to sing the whole song if the creative team tells you to continue (which is, of course, a great sign). Do your best to pick a song that's not hugely overdone like a current Broadway hit song but also not so off-the-radar that the creative team will never have heard it before, or will have heard it so rarely that they're sitting there thinking, *Where have I heard this song before?* because then they're too focused on the mystery of the song rather than the person singing it.

At an initial audition for a show, you will usually have free choice about what to sing, within reason. You'll want to select something that matches the vocal range of the role you're trying out for and something in a style that works with the show, but you don't have to pick a song that's actually from the show—that comes during callbacks, when you'll be asked to prepare a part or parts from the score.

It may be that you'll have some direction for the initial audition, too—the call may ask for you to prepare an up-beat, contemporary song, for example. You'd be amazed by how many people will ignore that and just sing whatever they feel shows off their voice best. Don't do this. There's a reason they're asking for that particular type of song. Give the creative team what they've asked for or they will believe that you won't follow directions once hired, either.

When you're singing, the temptation is often just to stand there and sing, using facial expressions, of course, but not really integrating yourself into the room. I want to encourage you to take a moment before singing, just like I encourage you to take a moment before your acting audition, and en-vision the same things—picture the set, the other actors, the lighting. Picture what time of day it is, what year, what season. Picture what just happened that made you want to start singing. Your song is a monologue set to music; you must know exactly what you're singing about. Again, even though audition times are short, casting professionals really don't mind the extra ten or twenty seconds it will take you to do this because it will likely result in a better performance.

The song "Popular" from *Wicked*—my big song for so many years—is also a song that's frequently used in auditions. Singers will often stand there smiling before the opening note is played and then just jump right into it . . . but they forget what's going on in Glinda's world when that song starts. What caused her to break into song? She has had a *vision*. She's checking out her roommate, Elphaba, and finally seeing some kind of potential in her. Suddenly, she feels so inspired to do something great—she's going to help Elphaba in the only way she knows how: through a makeover.

So before those opening notes, all of that has to be going through your mind. You're not staring off into the audience or at the casting director. You're not standing there waiting to sing. You're having this *moment* that can only be honored through bursting into song. Picture Elphaba there next to you. Picture the two beds, the lamps, the light bulb that's just gone off in your mind about how you have the power to fix this young lady. Think about how thrilled you are to get to work and how you first want to lay it all out for her so she will be just as excited as you are.

Then sing.

When you are working on your material, it helps to set up the space around you. Who are you singing to? Where are you? What just happened to make you go into your song? What do you want from the person you're singing to? You need to be able to answer all these questions.

Getting Feedback

Sometimes you'll leave an audition knowing you blew it, and it won't be any great surprise when you don't get called back or cast. But other times you may think you nailed it, and then, when you don't get the call, you're disappointed and wondering what went wrong. Was it that they just didn't like your singing, dancing, or acting? Was it that you were wrong for the part? Did they just like someone else better?

There was one time when I knew I had done so well at a callback that I was sure I had the part. I was already envisioning how I would go in and give my notice at *Wicked,* and they would be so happy for me . . . and then I got a call from my agent saying, "I'm sorry. They're not moving forward with you."

I was devastated. It took some time for me to let that go and remember all I had to be thankful for and that I should enjoy where I was. I never did find out just why they didn't choose me, and often, that's how it is—you'll never know. Casting directors don't owe you any explanation. But you're more likely to get some feedback if you have an agent. The agent can call and ask for you, and at least then you'll know if you repeatedly get word back that your skills are lacking or if it's just a matter of not being quite the right fit for roles. You can also try calling the casting agency afterward yourself if you went for an open call. Sometimes you'll get the feedback and sometimes you won't, but it's worth trying as long as you're not demanding or pushy about it.

After You're Cast

Hooray! You got the job! No matter how far along in your career you are, it's always a heart-racing moment of excitement when the call comes in to say that you've been cast. No need to play it cool—feel free to shriek to your agent and dance around in your living room. You've earned it! Now it's time to celebrate—and get to work.

Naturally, the kind of prep work you can do in a few days

is not the same as what you'll do to prepare for a part once you're cast. Both require labor. You've been cast because the powers that be believe you "get" the role and fit into it well, so that's a start! But you'll have to do more than that to get ready for your big opening performance.

It's important for you to understand what motivates a character to act as he or she does in every scene and every musical number. When you're in the ensemble, you may have more leeway to imagine your character's backstory and what's going on in his or her mind. When you have a principal role, there are normally a lot of clues in the script. You'll figure out most of what you need to know about your character there and then fill in the gaps with your imagination.

There are several techniques you can try when you're getting to know a character:

- **Write a character bio.** Write the bio from your character's point of view. How would he describe himself? How would she talk about her accomplishments, flaws, family, education, job, relationships, home, friends . . . ?

- **Interview your character.** Write down or think through a Q&A session with your character. Ask lots of "why" questions. *Why do you feel this way? Why did you do that? Why didn't you do that?* Try to get to know the character's backstory. How were they raised? Where did they grow up? What was their family like? What's their favorite color? What did they want to be when they grew up?

- **WWCD?** What would the character do? As you go through your day, you can take a page from the Method acting school of thought and ask yourself how your character would perform your everyday tasks. What would your character have for breakfast (and who would prepare it)? How would your character feel about your making small talk with your neighbors? What kind of driver would your character be? What time would your character wake up and go to bed? Would your character fall asleep easily or ruminate?

- **Research the role.** If this is not a new show, see how others have played the part. You don't need to play it exactly the same way, but if you can watch videos (or even better, see in person) other people playing the role, you may pick up on nuances you hadn't noticed before that you'll want to incorporate. It's funny how, years after playing a role, I often wish I could go back and play it again with newfound knowledge and experiences. It's amazing how many different takes there can be on one role.

Getting off-book quickly is a key to diving into your character. It's hard to fully settle in when you're still looking down at your script. Nothing replaces repetition when it comes to drilling lines, so keep practicing out loud—with a partner, if you can—until you could recite those lines in your sleep. Everyone appreciates an actor who puts in the time to learn the lines quickly; it's an essential skill in professional theatre. In school shows, you may get a month or more to learn your lines; on Broadway, you get a week or two.

THERE'S AN APP FOR THAT

There are a few apps that can help you practice and learn your lines, particularly useful when you don't have a patient partner to practice with. Check these out in your app store:

LineLearner (for iOS and Android)

Rehearsal Pro (for iOS)

RMS Sides (for iOS and Android)

Taking It in Stride

Every show has its blooper reel.

I was playing Nessarose in *Wicked,* and a friend of mine was brand new to the role of Boq. It was the dance scene, and he was supposed to wheel me out on stage and never let go of the wheelchair—particularly because it was a raked stage. Well, he got a little overly excited about his debut and lost track of what he was doing for a minute, and he let go of the handles.

I went rolling forward, right toward the orchestra pit. Slowly at first, but steadily. I was holding a prop in my hands, and I was determined not to break character and use my legs to stop the wheelchair from careening straight into the conductor.

"Boq," I said quietly. No response. *"Boq."* Then, finally, I said his real name.

He finally noticed my predicament and grabbed me just

in time, but in that instant, I realized I was so committed to this part that I was about willing to break my neck for it.

Other times there were mechanical issues (how very pedestrian to have to *walk* on stage when the bubble had technical difficulties!) or missed lines. Part of what the audience likes about live theatre is that there is this possibility—they don't necessarily expect perfection, but human moments that show that they're witnessing something real. You just have to keep working at it until you're comfortable ad-libbing, changing choreography on the spot, or doing whatever else it takes to get the show back on track. Don't be afraid to help feed a line or pick up a prop if someone is in trouble on stage. We're all in this together.

Talent gets your foot in the door, but doing the hard work of being prepared for your auditions, rehearsals, and performances makes it so much more likely that you'll be one of the lucky people who winds up with a successful long-term career.

Agents and Managers

Here's what people think is going to happen:

"I'm going to get to New York, send out my headshots and résumés, and find an agent, and that agent is going to handle all the casting stuff for me. I may have to wait tables or do other work in the meantime, but my agent will call with auditions and I'll just do whatever he says."

But the truth of the matter is this: *If* you get an agent, you're still going to be doing the bulk of searching for calls yourself. Agents have lots of clients and won't send you out for everything you're appropriate for; they will, of course, take calls from casting directors who have specifically requested you, and they'll watch whatever comes across their desk to see if you might be right for something, but you're still your best representative when it comes to finding work.

They're thinking about you part of the time during the day, nine to five. When they go home, they're not thinking about how to best make your dreams come true. Only you can do that.

You *have* to stay abreast of open calls and know what shows are coming down the pike. Then you can ask your agent to send you out for shows you think are well suited to you, or you can just show up at open calls if you don't get the response you need.

The Differences Between Agents and Managers

Agents and managers cover some of the same territory, but there are a few differences, at least in theory. An agent gets 10 percent of your earnings and is tasked with negotiating your contracts, getting you appointments, and watching for auditions that might be right for you.

Managers are supposed to be more hands-on and big picture; they may take a bigger commission (15 percent) in exchange for taking on fewer clients and paying more attention to each client's overall career goals. There's less vetting of managers; they're not licensed or regulated in any way and thus are not supposed to solicit work or negotiate contracts for their clients, but of course they do. Managers can also get you meetings with agents.

Do you need one or the other? I'd say you should endeavor to find an agent because that opens a lot of doors for you that you can't open on your own. I've had a few agents through the years as my career goals changed and as I saw who was and wasn't putting in effort for me. As far as both, though, that's a decision you'll have to weigh against the money you're giving up.

If you have both an agent and a manager, you're giving up 20–25 percent of your earnings on every project in perpetuity. What can be galling about it is if all the agent did was to make one phone call to negotiate a few points in a contract, and then for the next two years that you're in a show, 10 percent of every paycheck goes to that agent for that one phone call. Even worse is if you went to an open audition, got yourself cast, and now you're paying out 20–25 percent of your next two years' income to two different people who did nothing but make a phone call after the fact.

But on the flip side, they can get you jobs you wouldn't even have found out about on your own or get you private appointments for auditions at times when there are no open calls or you might otherwise sit around all day hoping to be seen and then get shut out. They can take care of sticky negotiations for you so that you don't have to develop any kind of contentious relationship with a producer. They can make sure you get a humidifier in your dressing room on tour or that you get weekly facials paid for if you're Elphaba and a makeup person is painting you green every night.

They can step in when you have a conflict or difficult situation and you need an advocate. They can be great cheerleaders for you and prop you up when you're doubting yourself. They can help you figure out where you fit into the industry and what kinds of roles you should be trying out for. In other words, there are lots of reasons agents earn their commissions—it's just that it's a gamble. Sometimes it'll feel like they more than earned their fee, and other times it'll feel like you're handing over part of your paycheck for no good reason.

Some agents and managers will also negotiate with you so that if you bring in work on your own, you won't owe a commission or you'll owe a reduced commission. I've never tried to argue that point because I feel like every time an agent gets a check from my work, it puts my name back in front of them and makes them think positively of me. When a client looks to cut their agents out of deals, I think it makes the agent less likely to push on their behalf next time. It's important to me that agents know I value their work so they'll get on the phone enthusiastically and talk me up to the casting director when I call to ask, "Can you get me an appointment for this?"

Agents get the descriptions of what a director is looking for, and while much of it is nonnegotiable, an agent can also make a case for you if there's something not quite fitting about it. For instance, if you're a little taller than what they want, or your hair is the "wrong" color (lots of people wear wigs on stage, anyway!), or if they want to see you at 1:00 but you have another audition and need a different time slot. They can even push back if a casting director has over-looked you, depending on their relationships in the busi-ness. A casting director might have counted you out based on what they know of your past performances. ("She's a dramatic actress, and this calls for humor," a casting direc-tor might say—and then it's up to your agent to say, "You haven't seen that side of her yet, but she's great at comedy. I think you should see her for this.") Agents can't argue every time for every person, or casting directors would get pretty tired of their calls, but they can do it when they feel it's legitimate. You want the agent on your side and ready to go to bat for you.

There are also times when an agent may send you on a call that they know isn't completely right for you just to get you in front of someone who hasn't seen you before. In this way, the agent is using the audition more like a showcase so the person may think of you for other projects.

Every time you go out for an audition or show up at a performance, you're a representation of not only your agent and manager but also the casting director who brought you in. All those people stand to look very good, or very bad, depending on how you do and your behavior. You can blow it with any of them by messing up: getting into fights, showing up late, forgetting your entrance, and so on. This is a business that isn't big on second and third chances, again because there's so much competition for every role. To stay working, you have to stay in the industry's good graces, which means doing your best consistently and never blowing off an opportunity because you think it's beneath you.

You can, of course, turn things down. If an agent sets up an audition for you and you can't or don't want to do it, you can call and explain why, but for the most part, you and your agent need to be on the same page about what you do and don't want to do, and your availability. When you're traveling, or you've booked other work, or you need to take time away, you have to let your agent know; even if you feel like the agent hasn't done anything for you lately, you don't know if they're sending out your headshot and résumé and just not getting hits. Don't let them waste their time if you're unavailable or interested in only some types of parts.

THE WHOLE AGENCY

• •

In some other creative fields, you sign with one particular agent at an agency. With acting, it's not like that; you sign with an entire agency. You may get to know one agent above others, but if that agent retires or leaves the company, you're still represented by the original agency (there are some cases when you can follow the subagent if you really want to). According to regulations, agencies need to have offices. A manager is more likely to be a lone wolf and can work from home or anywhere else.

Different Agents for Different Things

One of the big parts of my career in recent years is symphony concerts. When I told this to my current agency, they were up front in letting me know that they don't look for that type of work. That's fine, because it let me know that I was on my own for that part and I didn't need to pay a commission on it. So either I could find and negotiate that work on my own (which I do), or I could try to find another agent, manager, or attorney to specifically work on that type of work for me.

More commonly, though, the question comes up in terms of film and television. Some agencies are large and wide-reaching and can be reasonably expected to look for work for you in whatever areas you want—voiceover, commercials, dinner theatre, cruise ships, whatever. Others specialize in one or another, so you might have one agent for stage work, and a different agent for film and television, and a third one for voiceover work. It's important to establish up front and in contract form what's expected, though, so that you don't wind up in a situation later where you're expected to pay commissions to more than one agent on a single job.

Managers will likely expect commissions on everything you do in the entertainment industry, whether it's within their specialty or not. But not always.

Donna Vivino suggests that there are really two times in a performer's career when a manager is valuable: in the beginning when you have no contacts and need all the help you can get, and once you've *really* hit it big and have so much going on that you don't know how to juggle it all and need someone to direct your career for you so that you take advantage of only the best opportunities. If you're somewhere in between all that, you probably don't need a manager.

New York Agent?

One of the big questions I get when I teach workshops and master classes is whether or not my out-of-town students should get New York agents for Broadway, off-Broadway, and tour work. The real answer is that it depends on whether or not you're ready to move on a moment's notice.

Let's say you live in Chicago. You may be able to submit a tape for round 1 of auditions, but there will quickly come a point where you need to come in and be seen in person if the creative team likes you. A New York agent can set that up for you, but you won't get much notice and you can't consistently turn things down, or that agent will give up on you. So it depends on what you're doing and how ready you are to jump.

If you're a high school student, can you and do you want to leave school and spend a year or more being tutored or homeschooled? If you're in college, will your school let you pause your studies? Will you lose that semester's tuition?

If you have a family, another job, a house, pets, kids, how readily can you uproot yourself for something uncertain? You'd need to first travel to New York for an audition (and maybe more than one, because callbacks can go on for some time), then be ready to start rehearsals whenever the director says, "You're hired." That means hurrying to find local housing, which is rarely affordable.

But if your life is relatively free of commitments, and you're at a point where you're ready and able to drive or fly to New York with just a few days' notice, and this is your big goal, then sure—approach the New York agents. Agents in other cities are great for getting you work in regional theatres, locally filmed shows and commercials, and regional tours, but they're very unlikely to be connected to the Broadway and off-Broadway and national touring world. And that's fine while you're building a résumé and gaining experience; in most cases, that's just what I'd recommend until you finish with college. Stay in training, stay near your family, and make the big move only when you've hit that natural stage in your life. There's no need to rush it along.

Agentless

Don't wait until you have an agent to get started, and don't make it your main priority. My friend Michael McCorry Rose was in the ensemble of a Broadway show and still couldn't get an agent to even respond to his submissions!

"I sent twenty letters with headshots and résumés, several with personal recommendations, and I got zero responses. Finally, a friend of mine in casting who had seen me come in for several things said he would talk to an agency he was working with for me. I figured that would be great—maybe they would sign me. But no, they emailed me and said, 'In four months, we'll hold auditions. You can come then.'"

When he got there, he found himself in a room with about 150 other actors, all hoping to be signed. Fortunately, he was one of two who did get signed, but it can often seem just as hard to get an agent as it is to get booked on a big job. You can't wait for it; keep putting yourself out there while you're looking.

YOU SHOULDN'T BE SCARED
OF YOUR AGENT

A casting director friend of mine says that he's amazed by how many actors he knows tell him that they're scared to call their agent to ask for something or that they're worried their agent will drop them.

"If you're not comfortable with your agent and you're afraid they're going to drop you, that's not a good relationship to be in. What's the point? Just get out there on your own," he says. "Your agent is supposed to be your best champion."

Where to Find Legitimate Agents

Word of mouth is the best method. Don't be afraid to ask around. Befriend fellow actors and people in the industry and ask who they've worked with and whether or not they're happy. When you're in a show with someone and they mention that their agent is in the audience, ask for that introduction.

This doesn't apply to strangers or mentors, though. If you're new in town and trying to get to know fellow actors, it's not polite to ask them for agent referrals. Because I teach, I'm often asked if I'll refer students to my agent, and it's uncomfortable. As much as I'd like to help everybody, I can't vouch for people I haven't worked with in a show. My reputation is tied to anyone I recommend, and I don't want my agency to get tired of hearing that I'm sending masses of people their way without knowing they'd be a good fit.

I'm more than happy to help in other ways, though. Most of the pros you meet are glad to recommend classes, voice coaches, photographers, web designers, and the like and to give opinions on whether or not an audition is worthwhile, or what you should sing, or which headshot shows you off best, or things like that. We can help point you to mentors, and we can answer questions about how the business works.

We can also tell you whether or not we like our agency or other agents we've worked with—but it becomes an imposition when you ask for referrals before you've proven yourself on a professional level.

Aside from word of mouth, you can also try *Backstage*'s call sheet, www.backstage.com/resources/search/agent, which lists hundreds of agents in a format that's searchable by union affiliation (Screen Actors Guild–American Federation of Television and Radio Artists [SAG-AFTRA], Equity, and others), type of talent represented (theatre actors, film and TV actors, commercial actors, singers and musicians, voiceover artists, comedians, fashion and runway models, print models, and hosts and spokespersons), age range they represent, and office locations.

Big Agency or Small Agency?

There's no one-size-fits-all answer to this question, though I personally give preference to the major agencies. The upsides to being with a major agency are clear: more opportunities pass through their desks, and they may have more clout and more negotiating power. But the downside is that you may get lost in the crowd at a big agency.

When an agency has lots of superstar clients, they may not pay much attention to you, especially if you don't land something big with them quickly. You may also run into a problem with the agency representing too many people who are similar to you in looks or talents, which pits you against their other clients.

A smaller agency, or one that's newer to the business, may be able to give you more individualized attention—but the trade-off is that they may not have much standing in the industry and may not be able to get you appointments as easily.

You're not stuck with an agency forever, though. Agency contracts may be slightly different for non-Equity versus Equity actors. If you're an Equity actor, the initial term is limited to one year, at which time you can renew it or cancel the agreement if you're unhappy. Nonunion contracts are also often for one-year terms or can be negotiated down to that if the contract calls for a longer term. There can also be provisions that allow you to cancel if the agent hasn't found you work for several months (ninety days, according to Equity contracts), or if you haven't earned a minimal amount of money.

I also know some actors who've worked with agents without a formal contract; when the agent brings them work, the agent gets a commission, but there's no ongoing obligation between them.

If you decide to stop working with an agency, you will still owe an ongoing commission to the agency for projects they have submitted you for. According to Equity terms, you must terminate your contract in writing with a copy sent to Equity. Don't burn bridges; always offer an explanation for why you're terminating and resist the urge to make it personal—it's a business decision. If the agency isn't finding you the right work (or any work), then it's okay to move on and wish each other well.

How Do You See Me?

Sometimes when actors get an offer of representation, it's so exciting that they forget to ask questions. They just figure that if someone's interested, they'd better say yes quickly.

You need to know that you and your agency are on the same page about where you fit and how you want your career to go. Let's say you've done comedic work, but you also want to be sent out for serious dramatic roles. You have to find out if your agent sees you only as a comedic actor.

The easiest way to do that is to ask the question simply: "How do you see me? What kinds of roles would you send me out for?"

If you're not hearing what you want, make sure you say so.

"Well, I know that I do have improv experience, but that's not my only goal. I want to know that you'll push for me to be seen for straight plays, too."

The reverse is valid, too, of course—maybe you've done some heavy shows lately and are looking for lighter fare, but you know your résumé doesn't yet reflect what you want.

You'll have to gauge the reaction to determine if the agent will truly take your lead on this or if the agent has a vision for your career that's different from yours. The agent's main goal is for you to bring in a steady paycheck (for you and for them), but you may be more willing to take risks of dry spells in order to wait for roles that are really meaty or more up your alley. Try to determine this up front by having these kinds of conversations, even if they feel awkward at first. It's very rare that a talk like this would ever get heated.

Always remember that even though an agent has to choose you, they're still working for you and not the other way around. It's always valuable to get professionals' opinions on where you belong and what you can do to be more marketable, but not every agent is right for every performer—or right for them at every stage of their career.

Some agents are more conservative about following breakdowns and will send you out only if you match a description perfectly, whereas others take a looser approach and will try even if you're not quite a match. (Breakdowns do change, or get tossed out, if the creative team happens to fall in love with someone who isn't what they had originally envisioned.)

See if the approach aligns with your own; maybe you want to be sent out for everything, or maybe you'd feel uncomfortable showing up when you know you don't match a breakdown.

Above all, I'd talk to my fellow actors about their experiences with an agency before signing a contract. One person saying, "They didn't do much for me," shouldn't mean you have to turn down representation, but you want to be as informed as possible. What you hear may confirm your suspicions or give you more to think about. In the end, it's best to hold out and keep looking if you don't feel right about an agent.

"HIP-POCKET" REPRESENTATION

In rare cases, an agent may not sign you to an overall contract but may offer to "hip-pocket" you instead, which means a more limited agreement. That comes up in a few scenarios—it could mean that the agent sees you as having a specific skill or some kind of specialized talent or look that comes up rarely and would submit you only in those cases when it's called for. It could also mean one agent is on board with you, but others at the agency aren't convinced, so that agent submits you on a limited basis with the hopes of it being a successful trial. It can work in your favor, too, because it gives you a way of trying out the agent without committing to him or her.

Similarly, you may freelance for more than one agency. Some agencies allow this and some don't; you may strike an agreement (in writing or verbally) to have an agency represent you nonexclusively so that you owe commissions only on work they bring your way. They are not as invested in your career as they would be for signed actors (actors signed to an exclusive contract), but I also know people who like this type of noncommitted relationship. I do suggest that you get agreements in writing whenever possible so there's no question about either party's responsibilities.

Making Contact

When approaching an agent or manager, you send over your headshot and résumé, along with a very brief cover letter that says you're looking for representation (or new representation, if you're leaving another agency). Most agencies accept submissions by email at this point (one or two headshots and your résumé as a PDF file, preferably, to reduce the fear of viruses and to ensure the formatting you see on your end will look the same on their end; some agents will also look at video links).

Don't send submissions over weekends or holidays; they're likely to get ignored and then lost. When emailing, it's best to send during normal business hours. Then, about two to three weeks later, make a phone call if you haven't heard from them. They're just people; so many of my actor friends can get up on stage in front of thousands of people, but they're afraid to pick up a phone to say, "I sent over my headshot and résumé a couple of weeks ago and just wanted to know if you've had a chance to review it yet, and if I can come in for a meeting."

You're selling yourself. Be willing to be your own best advocate and take those chances. They get tons of submissions, and some do fall through the cracks; remind them that you're around and that you're worth their time.

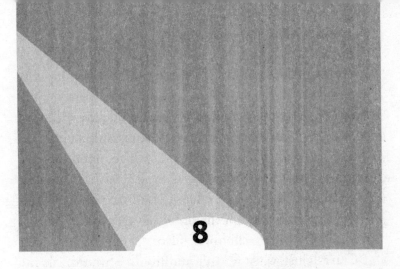

8

Video Auditions

Each year at our Destination Broadway workshop in New York City, we offer parent sessions in addition to the classes for students, and one of our most popular parent topics is about how to prepare video auditions, also known as *self-tapes*.

So much has changed since I began in this business—which wasn't *that* long ago!—and video auditions are a huge time-saver for both actors and casting professionals. You'll find that many directors for both live theatre and film and television welcome video auditions as a first step. It's never the final step, but it can help them to narrow down the field quickly so they can call in just the people who they think best fit the open roles.

This is especially good for people who live outside of New

York or Los Angeles; you can submit your tape from any-where as long as you're willing to travel for in-person audi-tions if you get the call. At that point, you'll know you're not just spinning your wheels; there may be many people called in, but you'll know that you have a real shot and that the director liked your video.

The funny thing for me when I was living in New York is that I was often just a block or two away from the casting office and was told to submit a video.

"Can't I just walk in and audition?" I would ask my agent—but no. They wanted videos first regardless of where performers lived. It keeps their budget down (no need to re-serve audition space) and enables them to fast-forward and skip around quickly without hurting anyone's feelings when they decide someone's not right for the role. It's also useful if the director can't be in New York City for the auditions. And it benefits performers because it means you don't have to plan around an audition that may take up half your day and require you to pay for transportation. The main draw-back is the lack of feedback and body language . . . usually you can get a sense of whether or not the creative team liked you or adapt to changes they request when you're in the room, but you don't get to see anyone's face when they're watching your self-tape, so you may always wonder whether it went well or not. And if you're the kind of person who's more energetic in front of an audience, you may have qualms about tapes.

One thing that should put your mind at ease is that these are not meant to be professionally filmed in any way. It's not even necessary to have someone film you; the vast majority of video auditions are done with a cell phone set up by the actor in his or her home, on a tripod or other steady surface. You're even discouraged from getting too fancy because there are often limits to file sizes when submitting; filming with a DSLR camera may bloat the video file past the size limit.

When I was on tour, I would film my videos in hotel bathrooms. They almost always have great lighting and acoustics! I thought it was my special secret until I asked my friends on tour to help by reading opposite me or holding my phone to film me, and they would all chime in, "I knowwwww! I love filming in hotel bathrooms!"

There are two parts of the tape: the *slate* and the *reading*.

The Slate

The slate is your introduction, where you say your name and a few brief words of introduction. It's not a time to get wordy and creative; it's also not a time for you to be in character. If you're under eighteen, you say "Hi" or "Hello," then your full name, age, and height, and the role or show you're auditioning for. If you're eighteen or older, it's just a greeting, then your name and the role or show you're auditioning for ("Hi, I'm Hannah Smith, and I'm reading for the role of Susan"). You may also be instructed to mention your agency's name. That's it. No one will kill you for adding in a few extra words, but they really don't want you getting cutesy or using this as your place to be different—they have tons of tapes to get through, and this part is just to identify you and get a quick glance at you.

You may film this as a separate scene or all in one take with your audition. Show some enthusiasm and friendliness, but aside from that, don't let this part get you too worked up.

One thing you can do is to frame this part differently from your audition. We'll talk about framing in a minute—it varies based on what type of audition it is—but for your slate, you can show the casting director the "other side." You can film your slate as a close-up shot if the rest of it will be a full-body shot, or vice versa.

The Audition

This is where you'll perform the sides you've been given. You may record just one version, or you may do a second version in a different fashion if you want to show two different ways you can perform the part—only if it's a principal part that really does have more than one distinct way it could reasonably be played. If you have an agent who's submitting the tape for you, the agent can make the decision whether to submit both takes or just one. You need to be able to trust your agent to make that call.

Most of the time, just one version is needed, and if you get the call to come in for an in-person audition, you can show off your versatility.

You'll need to ask someone to read the lines that aren't yours in the script. That person should be standing next to the camera so you'll have a natural place to look that's close to the camera, but not right *at* the camera (which is creepy!). Some people try to have the other lines prerecorded . . . but don't. It doesn't work out well. You really do need a live person in the room to do the scene with you. And that person shouldn't overshadow you; make sure he or she isn't speaking too loudly or dramatically. You're the one auditioning, not them.

Background, Clothes, and Lighting

You'll want your background to be as plain and non-distracting as possible. A solid-color wall or curtain is great. If you don't have a large enough area that's solid, then you may hang a bedsheet behind you. (Make sure it's ironed or it gets highlighted when lit.) You don't want any clutter showing in the background.

Ideally, go with a subdued color background (like blue, gray, brown, or taupe) rather than stark white, just because white walls are rarely flattering to skin tones. You also don't want to wear white or anything with stripes (it creates an optical illusion on camera) or logos. Keep clothing simple and appropriate to the character, though don't try to wear a "costume."

You'll also want to make sure you're well lit, which means that your face isn't dark or in shadow, but that it also doesn't look like someone is shining a flashlight in your face. Facing a window with the shades open can provide great light, or floor lamps can supplement, or you might want to invest in a simple lighting kit. Don't be afraid to get creative—take shades off lamps, and try different bulbs and configurations until you look bright and natural.

Try to have one light behind the camera that makes your eyes "pop." It can dramatically change how well your eyes convey emotion.

Framing

My friend Clifton Samuels, a veteran of Broadway, touring, film, and television, gives advice for how to frame your shots for different types of auditions. Keep in mind that all of these are filmed horizontally ("landscape" mode):

Film/TV

- Comedy (which is always double-spaced in the sides): Frame the shot from your belly button to a little above your head.

- Episodic: Chest to a little above your head.

- Feature film: A little tighter than your chest—head, shoulders, and just below.

Musical Theatre

- Full body, head to toe. A theatre audience doesn't need the same close-ups as a TV audience would, and your body movements have to be bigger for theatre.

Keep in mind that none of these are strict rules—they're guidelines. In the case of the hotel bathroom videos I filmed, it was impossible to get full-body framing, so we did the best we could.

Sound

Be very aware of the background noises that may intrude on your audition and do what you can to control them—

air-conditioning (turn it off just before you record), dogs barking (be sure they're occupied), phone ringing (turn off the ringer), a roommate walking in (put up a "Quiet, please—I'm recording" sign). It can be so frustrating to be just about done with a great take and then have a friend ring the doorbell or a fire truck come through the neighborhood.

You may have to time your taping so you're doing it when traffic is low or people are asleep, or you may have to find a space outside of your house to tape if you're unable to get peace and quiet. You can rent studio space for forty-five minutes to an hour for about fifty dollars, and they can provide you with a reader.

Most cell phones today do a good job of recording without needing an additional microphone for acting calls, but you may want to add a clip-on body mic for singing auditions. Just make sure your voice is clear and loud enough when you play it back.

BEFORE YOU PUT IT ON YOUTUBE

Be sure you've checked your instructions. Sometimes directors don't want videos posted publicly because scripts are meant to be kept secret. If you've signed a nondisclosure form, it's likely you're not supposed to post the video.

Common ways to send audition tapes are as Vimeo or WeTransfer files, or private YouTube links.

But It's Not Perfect

Clifton advises people to do about four takes, not endless tries to make it "perfect." If you can memorize all of it, great, but when you have a very short turnaround, that may not be possible, and it's okay to make yourself cue cards for guidance. Make sure you have the beginning and ending down cold, though, and don't keep glancing down at a script in your lap. Even though it can work okay in person, it's really distracting on video to see someone's eyelids again and again.

Be aware of your pace and timing. If you get a line slightly wrong, though, keep going. "They don't care if it's perfect to the letter of the script," Clifton says. "Better to be wrong in words and right in essence. You watch humanity. Don't stop mid-scene to correct yourself; human moments are good."

The more you try to make a take "perfect," the more likely it is to appear over-rehearsed and self-conscious and unreal. You *do* want to practice and be prepared, but you don't want to orchestrate every eye blink. Allow room for some spontaneity on camera. Don't watch every take before filming another one, or you're likely to obsess about each tiny piece. If you can't commit to stopping after four takes, at least set a reasonable time limit for yourself.

In the "Behind the Scenes" specials for *Stranger Things,* you can see each of the kids' original self-taped auditions. While Gaten Matarazzo's is pretty smooth and high quality, several of the others are . . . less so. One that stands out is Finn Wolfhard's; in his slate, he says, "I'm Finn Wolfhard, and I'm sick," before going into his scene. The shot is a little blurry, and he's sitting on his bed . . . and he got one of the starring roles!

The creators laugh about this, pointing out how they want this to be a lesson for hopeful actors: You can submit an imperfect tape from your bedroom while sick and still wind up with the part if your acting skills are on point.

Depending on Tapes

If your goal is to work in film and TV, self-tapes are even more the norm. However, if musical theatre is your bag, then you shouldn't get overly reliant on tapes as a means not to leave your hometown. There are many, many opportunities that call for you to be in New York City right at that moment—even to make a tape!

For instance, Cesar was on a recent call with a director of a new Broadway show at 8:30 a.m., and the director told him that they'd just lost one of their actresses for the show. They needed to recast the part immediately, and he didn't know what to do.

"I have half an hour free at 4:30. I can get girls here and put them on tape and send them to you by the end of the day," Cesar said. And that's what he did—he didn't consider anyone who wasn't in town that day. He called in three women to sing songs from their books that afternoon and sent the tapes to the director. The director immediately liked one of the women.

"Do you want to make her an offer?" the casting director asked.

"Yes, let's do that."

And just like that, this woman booked a Broadway show based on an impromptu taped audition that day. No waiting around all day at an EPA, no callbacks, no learning a song from the show, no wondering weeks later if she would get the call. It all happened that fast.

It can definitely be a big commitment to move to New York, especially if you're from a small town far away, but it's very hard to get a career launched if you're not at those calls in person all the time, meeting people in the industry. If you're not there already, get there as soon as possible.

9

Lessons on Persistence

By now, you've gotten the idea that this business is full of rejections. Just about everyone thinks they're going to be the exception to that rule and have a career that takes off right away and stays steady, but just about everybody is wrong.

It really does often feel like a "last man standing" game. You can go on auditions for years without ever getting your big break, but then one day, you walk in the room and you're exactly what the director is looking for. I know several people who didn't truly come into their own for a decade or more.

When people told me early on in the business that it's about who you know, I threw away that thought entirely. *Talent will always win out in the end,* I thought. But after all this time as a working actor, I can say that my outlook on that has changed. You do clearly need to be talented—very talented—to make it in this business, but once you hit a certain level of talent, it's hard to judge who's *more* talented than someone else; it's more a matter of taste and style. Who's more talented: Christine Ebersole or Bernadette Peters? I don't know; they're both legends with very different styles. They're not interchangeable, so it's hard to value one over the other. Same with other professional-caliber talents; it's not just about how well you sing and dance but about your energy, personality, and everything else that sets you apart from everyone else in the room.

But about that "who you know" thing: It is important. It *is*. Luckily, you can know people, too. So much of it is about repetition. A casting director may not remember you the second or third time he sees you, but by the tenth time? Much more likely. At that point, you're developing more of a rapport, making some small talk, and, with any luck, getting some feedback. When you get the sense that a particular director, producer, or casting director likes you, make sure your agent (or you) gets you in front of that person again and again until it clicks. Don't be afraid of being seen *too* many times by the same person, and don't think that just because someone hasn't cast you yet means they don't want to.

Sometimes it clicks in ways you didn't expect—it's not always about the big Broadway role.

The story of how I got involved with *The Drowsy Chaperone* is a bit winding. One day early in my career, I got a call from my agent telling me that a casting director who knew and liked me wanted me to be the reader for a new Broadway show.

Just like the time I called my parents all excited because I thought I was playing a character named Swing, this time I thought I was being cast as some kind of narrator. I was thrilled and didn't ask many questions on that phone call. The truth was a little anticlimactic but still a cool job: The reader is the person who reads whatever part is opposite the auditioner's character in the sides. So I was hired to read both male and female parts, depending on who walked into that audition room—a fun challenge.

Readers are hired both for theatrical productions and for film and TV. Being the reader is another fantastic opportunity for several reasons, but mostly because 1) it lets you hear what the creative team says about each auditioner after they leave, which gives you great insights, and 2) it allows that creative team to see you all day long for one or more days.

One of the biggest lessons I took away from it was that you can easily stand out from the crowd just by really knowing the material. Often, the director would ask actors to try the reading a different way, which is really a test to see how well they could take direction.

"It's a little too serious. She doesn't take things that seriously," the director would say, and then the actress would try again.

It surprised me how few actors truly took direction well, and what I noticed time and again was that the ones who succeeded were the ones who were mostly off-book—they didn't have to worry about remembering lines or reading, so they could focus on changing it up as the director wanted. The ones who were glued to the script wound up reading it mostly the same way the second time around or just floundering. Maybe they were making subtle changes that felt big to them, but live theatre isn't subtle like film is. When a director asks for a change, that change should be clear. Make a strong choice and go with it. If there's a choice in your mind between taking a risk or playing it safe, take the risk.

Bobby agrees with my observation, saying that when he gives notes during an audition, "about 70 percent of the time, they don't take direction." Sometimes, he said, they even just give attitude as if the note is stupid and they know better. But you're performing for an audience, not for a mirror, and sometimes the creative team can see or hear things that you can't—or is testing you to see if you'll be easy to direct.

I think part of the problem is people getting numb to the audition process; there are so many auditions and so much to learn that they don't work hard enough each time to prepare. Maybe it's that they get so used to rejection that they feel like it's not worth it to put in too much effort—but that's your job! You have to care each time, and you have to show that you're taking your work and the creative team's time seriously, not just rely on coasting by because of your talent or résumé.

There may even be little things you're doing that you have no idea you're doing until someone points them out to you. Maybe every time you act surprised, you raise your eyebrows so far that it turns your forehead into a mass of wrinkles, which looks weird. Asking you to take the surprise down a notch could be a response to that.

I wasn't at *The Drowsy Chaperone* call to audition myself,

and you can't go in with the expectation that this will lead to an audition, but it did for me. At the end of about two weeks of reading, the director turned to me and said, "You've been great here. I love your energy. We have a little time left; would you like to do a song for us?"

Well, of course I would! Afterward, they thanked me, but I didn't get the call I hoped would come. Later, they had to hire some replacement actors and called me back to read again. By that time, I'd been cast in *Wicked,* but my weekdays were still mostly free, so I could take on the job. They were so sweet and supportive of me when they learned I'd gotten my first big break. Still, after it was over, I didn't hear from them again . . . for a year.

A year later was when they were mounting the national tour, and I got a call telling me I didn't even need to audition: They wanted me to be the dance captain. Again, you just never know where something is going to lead as you build up those relationships. The director didn't mention my talent (though, of course, I hope he thought I was very talented!); he remembered my "energy" in the room.

I think it's so important for actors to bring positive energy into every situation they're in. Give more than is expected of you whenever you can and cultivate positive relationships with everyone around you. You want people to smile when you walk into the room because they know you're going to bring the mood up, not down.

MAKE THE CALL
• •

One of the biggest "looking back now, I wish I'd
known..." kinds of lessons I've learned is that you really
can stick your neck out and ask for the things you
want in this business. I didn't even know there was
such a thing as a "reader" gig before I did it, but
knowing about it now, I would totally encourage young
actors to call up casting agencies to offer up their
services as readers. You can just call and speak to an
assistant and say, "Hi! My name is So-and-So, and I'm an
actor looking for some extra work. I would love to be a
reader if you have any openings."

It's not the kind of job an agent will seek out for
you, and they won't take a commission from it, but you
can also ask your agent (if you have one) to make a
couple of calls on your behalf in this way. Ultimately,
they should want you to make a living at your craft,
and they should understand that getting you in front
of creative teams is always a good idea, so it's okay to
ask them to use their relationships to your benefit.
Don't wait for people to call you. Reach out to whom-
ever you know in the business and let them know
you're available not only for shows but for side jobs,
too. Be proactive and brave; you have to pay the bills,
and ultimately, you're always going to be your best
representative.

The same goes for meeting professionals in environments other than auditions. If you find out there's a
producer or director in the audience of a show you're

in, unless you're explicitly told not to, take the opportunity to introduce yourself afterward. It's your life and your career at stake; take the chances. Never be abrasive, but always be bold.

Fifteen Years

When I got my seventy-two nos in a row, it felt like for*ever*. In actuality, it was just a matter of months, not years, from the time I moved to New York to the time I was cast in a Broadway show. Looking back now, that was fast! I have friends who've paid their dues far longer than I did— including one who had been pounding the pavement for fifteen years until she got her big Broadway break, coincidentally also in *Wicked*!

There are people who get lucky quickly and land big shows right away, but that's not the norm. Most of us do pay our dues in many ways: performing wherever anyone will cast us; studying, studying, studying our craft; getting up at the crack of dawn to warm up our voices only to stand on line at open calls, trading shifts at the day job to make it to another callback that doesn't pan out . . . it really is work, and when you're in the thick of it, it can start to feel hopeless. You have to find ways to dig deep within yourself to keep going, assuming this is really what you want to do and you can't imagine your life without it.

If that's you, then you remind yourself that this is a marathon, not a sprint. The doors that are meant to open for you will open for you. The doors that stay closed just weren't your doors. It's up to you to keep going until you find one that's yours. When you start getting callbacks, you'll know that you're getting closer to your door.

Everyone's path is different, and you won't know yours until you're already deep into it. British actor Alex Sharp was rejected at every major drama school in the UK. That might have been enough to discourage some students from continuing trying to be an actor, but instead he packed up and moved to the United States and auditioned at Juilliard, where he was accepted. Just a year after his graduation, in 2015, he won a Tony Award for his performance in the play *The Curious Incident of the Dog in the Night-Time*. When he was nominated, he said to *Business Insider,* "It's nice to know that there might be some kid getting rejected from a big drama school this year who might now realize it's not the end."

The Myth of the Overnight Success

The media loves a good overnight success tale. The problem is they're usually stretching the truth quite a bit, and it's not healthy for people to think that this is the way the business actually works.

When you see lots of stories about people coming up out of nowhere—as if they just landed in New York and *poof,* they're starring on Broadway—it can add to the demoralizing feeling of getting rejected.

If they all did it so quickly, I must be terrible, you might think. But don't!

More often than not, those "overnight successes" were doing quite a bit before they finally had their breakthrough role. They were studying, auditioning, and performing like everyone else. They just hadn't had their *big* part yet. But there is normally a progression; just because you hadn't heard of someone before doesn't mean they didn't go on a hundred auditions and spend four years studying in college (and community theatre and summer stock in high school), plus ensemble roles on tour or entertaining on a cruise ship . . . the media likes the glamour of the end result without showing everything it took to get there.

When Sutton Foster played Millie in *Thoroughly Modern Millie* on Broadway, newspaper after newspaper gushed about the "newcomer" who had come out of nowhere to win a Tony Award and become Broadway's new "It Girl." What they failed to recognize was that Sutton wasn't a newcomer at all; she'd been a professional Broadway and touring actress since 1994, and prior to that, she was on *Star Search* and had done lots of performing off Broadway. It wasn't even her first "big" role—back in 1994, she had understudied for both Sandy and Rizzo in *Grease* on Broadway and then played Sandy in the national tour. She was a hardworking actress who had more than paid her dues by the time she tried out for *Thoroughly Modern Millie* in 2000.

She had gone to an out-of-town audition for Millie but wasn't cast in the role, so she asked her agent to call and ask if they'd consider her for the understudy. They said yes. She turned down playing Éponine in *Les Misérables* on Broadway—a role she'd already played on tour—to play Millie's understudy at La Jolla Playhouse in San Diego, a first stop for many Broadway shows; twenty-eight of their productions have transferred to Broadway. She explained that she was just "ready for something different." Sutton was supposed to be in the ensemble, but when *two* original lead actresses had to drop out (Kristin Chenoweth turned it down for a TV deal, and Erin Dilly got sick and also had to leave just before tech rehearsals), Sutton stepped into the role. So when she won the Tony in 2002, she'd already been busting her butt for many years in productions around the country. This was *not* an "overnight success" but a positive trajectory that finally led to a role that gave her name recognition.

I want newer actors to understand that reality, because otherwise it's so tempting to think that either 1) this business is going to be easier than it is, when a "newcomer" can just drop in out of nowhere and win Broadway's biggest award, or 2) that you're doing something wrong if you don't hit it big right away.

What's important is that you keep getting out there and keep trying and keep improving, because there are people who will "get" you. It's important not to try to twist yourself into a pretzel changing your persona for every director you meet; just keep being you so that they get to know who you are and where they can place you. Often you don't know how close you are until you get that big call.

#TONYSSODIVERSE

One of the positive trends over the last few years is the rise in casting minorities. Until just a few years ago, about 80–85 percent of all actors cast in Broadway plays and musicals were white. A group called the

Asian American Performers Action Coalition sprang up when an Asian actor brought up a topic on Facebook about the lack of roles available to him, and other Asian actors chimed in to agree that the lack of diversity was a problem. But then came an upward trend, with shows like *Hamilton* and *On Your Feet!* As of 2016, 35 percent of all roles went to minority actors. Compared to the Oscars, which are often criticized for being overwhelmingly white (leading to the hashtag #OscarsSoWhite), the Tonys have looked far more representative of the actual diversity of actors. People who couldn't find roles a few years ago now can, showing again that sometimes it's just a matter of hanging in there long enough.

Dry Spells

We *all* have them. It's hard enough getting your first or second big break, but the thing is, you're asked to prove yourself over and over in this business, showing you're still relevant and still talented. Sometimes the roles just aren't there for you. Sometimes you're in an awkward stage where you're too old to play the ingénue roles but too young for the mom roles. Sometimes it's just plain bad luck and there's really no explanation.

The problem is that you can get psyched out by it all and lose your confidence in yourself, which can become a self-fulfilling prophecy. When you're feeling low and desperate, it's hard to come across well at an audition.

My friend Christy Altomare is a great example of the rocky nature of this business. She went to the University of Cincinnati College–Conservatory of Music as a musical theatre major at the same time I was there, but she was rarely cast in lead roles at school. In fact, she had to create her own show to graduate because she hadn't been cast enough to fulfill her performance requirements. At the end of her senior year, she participated in the school's showcase in New York, singing a song from *Spring Awakening.* She knew it was risky because there were few rock musicals around at the time, but it paid off for her immediately: The casting director for *Spring Awakening*'s first national tour was in the audience and invited her to audition.

She ended up getting cast as the lead, and it was a thrilling experience. Afterward, she did regional and off-Broadway work, playing opposite Derek Klena in a revival of *Carrie,* and then booked *Mamma Mia!* on Broadway. It was a surprisingly smooth start to her career—she knew that most people had to pay their dues more than that, but she was booking one gig after another. After a year, she decided to move on, figuring it was smart for her career to be open to new opportunities.

Except that there were almost no new opportunities.

Inexplicably, it seemed like work was just drying up for Christy. She wasn't getting any calls. She switched agencies. Her manager kept saying she was "trying," but she wasn't getting appointments. Having been in that situation, I know how demoralizing that can be. All of us have these dry spells where we wonder, *Is it me? Did I do something wrong? Am I not talented enough anymore? Have I lost my spark?* Especially after such a promising start, you can feel like yesterday's news . . . like the bands from the 1990s that no one cares about anymore except when they appear on a "Where They Are Now" list in some tabloid magazine.

Three years went by like this, and Christy was lucky that she'd been so frugal—she'd saved up enough from touring and Broadway that she was able to live off her savings. She had made peace with herself at some point, deciding that she would love herself and be proud of herself even if she wasn't acting anymore. Finally, after all that time, two opportunities came through at once.

She got appointments for the shows *Anastasia* and *Sign of the Times* on the same day—and then was booked for a final callback for *Sign of the Times* on the same day she found out she'd landed the lead in *Anastasia* for its out-of-town tryout. Although it was contracted that she would play the role if it made it to Broadway, the truth is that that's not always honored, and producers could easily buy her out of her contract.

But she *did* make it to Broadway and starred opposite Derek Klena again! In 2017, she was voted the Star of the Year by fans on Broadway.com.

That's why you have to remember that rejection isn't final. Even if you weren't the star of your school or college program, or even if you have a slow start, that doesn't mean you won't still end up somewhere great. Different people hit their stride at different times.

TV Talent Shows

Shows like *America's Got Talent* and *American Idol* are the latest in a long line of televised talent shows (*Star Search* launched in 1983 and went on for more than a decade, and *Showtime at the Apollo* started in 1987). It's true that they've launched several careers and at least boosted some others. People like Britney Spears, Beyoncé, Jennifer Hudson, Kelly Clarkson, Justin Timberlake, and Harry Styles all appeared on television talent shows before they got famous.

Sometimes these show producers like to make it sound like the contestants really have been plucked out of nowhere and that this is their first big shot. The contestants act wide-eyed and amazed as if they've never had an audience clapping for them before. But the trend lately has been toward more realism, and I'm so glad for that.

So many people who've been on these shows already have careers—they've been backup singers for recording artists, or they've had a record deal that didn't go anywhere, or they've done national tours. Jennifer Hudson was a church and community theatre performer who went on to entertain on Disney cruises when *American Idol* first began. She was already signed to an independent record label, but they let her out of her contract so she could audition.

I have nothing particularly against shows like these, but I hope young performers don't get too caught up in them. The truth is that they're even more competitive than most Broadway show auditions, and even those who uproot their lives and become finalists on the shows normally wind up going back to exactly what they were doing before. A very small percentage wind up with recording contracts or Broadway shows as a result of the show, so I worry that people get unrealistic ideas of what they can achieve if only they get a spot in front of the judges. Consider the case of "subway singer" Mike Yung, who earned a spot on *America's Got Talent* after a YouTube video of him singing "Unchained Melody" went viral. His house went into foreclosure while he was on the show, and despite being a fan favorite, he didn't make it to the show's finals. He's back singing in the New York subways again. Producers love to sell the fantasy that everyone's life is about to change and that all the people on the show will have their dreams come true, but it's not realistic in the vast majority of cases. Even *winning* a show like that hasn't always meant a successful career.

So, sure, audition if you want to, but I believe there are better uses of your time.

KEEP IT MOVING

One of Donna Vivino's best tips for dealing with the constant emotional ups and downs of auditions is to keep busy so that you won't have time to dwell. She always schedules something after an audition so she'll have a place to go and something to do.

Dropping Out of the Competition

In the dressing room, actors often talk about what auditions they're going on. Remember that even while someone is in a major show, they're still auditioning for others all the time—you have to, because you never know when your show is going to close, or if your contract will be renewed, or if you'll get tired of playing the same role for long stretches. During the week, auditions are normally from 10:00 a.m. to 5:00 or 6:00 p.m., so you can be in a show and still audition as usual. You'll hear the banter about which auditions are happening, and it can be easy to feel jealous when you find out someone booked an audition for a part that feels right for you.

Why didn't my agent send me out for that? you'll think, and it can send you into a downward spiral. *I know that casting director. Why didn't he call me? Doesn't he like me? Did I just get overlooked? Maybe he doesn't like me after all . . .*

Then you might call your agent and mention it. "Hey, I know they're doing auditions for *Miss Saigon.* Can you send me out for it?"

"We did."

"Oh."

Then it stings in a different way, because you've learned that you were turned down without even being seen. You'll also find that sometimes you're turned down for reasons that feel very unfair—like the time I went on an audition and the director took one look at my résumé and said in a disparaging way, "Oh, you're a Glinda."

He didn't look at me again, and it felt like he wasn't listening to my audition at all; he had already predetermined that I was "a Glinda," which meant that in his mind, I wasn't capable of playing a serious role.

There is a danger in getting typecast, which is why as you gain more and more credits, you might want to edit your résumé to show variety and leave out roles that are very similar to one another. But for the most part, you just soldier on and keep trying until you land where you're meant to land.

It's refreshing to me when actors *don't* talk about their auditions. We all understand that we're doing it, and we know that we're in competition with one another if we look and sound remotely similar, and that can make this an ugly business if you let it get to you. You spend your time backstage thinking, *Why her? Why not me?* or wishing someone would be quiet about their big callback that you didn't get.

At some point, you have to let go of the competition. It's hard to bond with people when you're in this tightrope walk of trying to outdo one another, and it creates tension and bad feelings when you're comparing yourself to others. Practice cultivating the thought that you're where you're meant to be and that each person's path is different. You will get the roles that are meant for you; they will get the roles meant for them. All that matters is that you keep working in some capacity so that you can survive and still do what you love.

Resist the urge to internalize other people's good news as bad news for you. Be happy for people when they land roles—even the roles you wanted. Keep moving. Keep getting yourself out there. For as long as it's your dream, never give up.

10

The Business of You

Even though it may feel like the last thing you want to be is a businessperson, you have to recognize this: Acting is a business. That's why they call it show *business* and not show *kidding around*. But seriously!

If you want to act as a hobby on the side and not worry about making it your career, that's fine, but assuming this is what you want to do as your main line of work, you have to remember that even though it's fun, you have to treat it as a business. You are the brand. Just about every day, you have to be out there building and selling your brand. Your talent is the product, and you have to convince people that they need your product more than they need anyone else's product that day. That's another way to maintain a little professional distance; it's not personal. If you were selling minty toothpaste and someone said, "No, thanks. I don't really need that toothpaste today," or "Thanks, but I like gel better than paste," you wouldn't be hurt. You'd understand that you should just move on to someone else who might need your toothpaste.

Your first order of business is to figure out what your brand is.

Who do you want to be in this business? What are you really good at? (For musical theatre, are you a dancer who sings or a singer who dances/moves well? Pick one. Just one.) What types of parts suit you? What excites you? What doesn't thoroughly excite you but still would be okay to pay the bills when you can't find work doing the stuff that *does* excite you?

Performing jobs are all about supply and demand. While it may be cool to do experimental theatre written by a playwright no one's ever heard of before, how many people do you think are going to pay for those tickets? That's what it comes down to: Will large numbers of people pay a good amount of money to see a show, and then will they tell others about it, and will they come back and see it again? Then you have a marketable show. You need to be part of those opportunities.

For the most part, people go to see shows they've heard of before—either because they're classic shows that have been performed all over the place, or because they're newer shows that have gotten great reviews in major media and won awards. Small theatres taking bigger risks and putting on shows that people are unfamiliar with may survive on grants, but it's unlikely for you to be able to make a living performing in them.

Commercial theatre is what we call any theatre that aims to draw a mass audience and make a profit. That, along with film/TV, commercials, and the like, are where you're most likely to earn a real paycheck. You may encounter a bit of snobbery from people who think commercial theatre is "selling out" and that experimental theatre and nonprofit theatre with more highbrow artistic goals is where it's at. But you can't do your craft as anything but a hobby if people aren't buying tickets. Snobbery is silly. The objective is to get people into the seats so you can keep doing what you love.

Lessons and Workshops

Having the right teachers can help you find your path. I've seen people with what I would consider mediocre talent end up really shining after taking high-level classes with people who know how to bring out the best in others.

First, let me say that everyone needs a vocal coach. People sometimes think it sounds like an insult. "Why do I need to take voice lessons? I have natural talent!" Or, "I already took voice lessons when I was a teen. I'm finished now."

This was something even Céline Dion went through. She was already a famous child star in Québec when a talk show host asked her on the air if she wanted to take voice lessons and she was downright *offended* by the question. She'd never taken lessons and she already had a recording contract. But taking voice lessons isn't just about learning how to sound better; it's also about learning how to sing with proper technique to get the maximum sound without hurting your voice. People who don't learn technique are much more likely to end up with vocal injuries that can stunt or end their careers. Céline was a bestselling artist when she humbled herself and realized that she also needed vocal coaching if she wanted to be able to sing for the rest of her life. She's a great example of someone who cared enough to work with vocal experts and as a result has seen her career continue to soar for decades beyond some of her contemporaries who blew out their voices early on.

My friend Donna was doing eight shows a week in *Hairspray* on Broadway when she started losing her voice regularly. She went to an ear, nose, and throat doctor, and he said, "You have some swelling that could turn into nodules. I want you to stop talking. Have you thought about taking voice lessons?"

She was lucky that this ENT knew all about singers.

"It's one thing to do *Les Mis* when you're a kid—you sing one song and you're done—but it's another to be in the ensemble singing almost three hours a night eight times a week, and maybe you don't have the technique to do that. Maybe you're singing right 80 percent of the time, but 20 percent you may not be, and now that's catching up with you."

Donna started studying with Joan Lader, a renowned vocal coach I worked with for ten years, who works with singers and actors with injured voices as well as coaching top talent from Broadway, opera, pop, and rock. It's not easy to get in with Joan; she's in high demand and mostly works on referral, coaching people like Patti LuPone and Kristin Chenoweth. Donna's doctor had referred her. What Joan learned was that Donna was speaking improperly even more than singing improperly. Donna trained and learned about the importance of vocal rest and was soon back on track. After that, Donna continued taking ongoing lessons with one of Joan's protégés. Then, when she was cast as Elphaba in *Wicked,* she called on Joan again, knowing that this role was spectacularly demanding.

"Elphaba? I've got you," she said. She had worked with other Elphabas and understood the need for intensive technique to handle belting out those songs every night.

Even while I played Glinda, I looked forward to my weekly lessons with Joan. I was in her studio every Tuesday. And it's important to keep training even when you're not actively in a show. Serena Williams doesn't practice her swing only when she has a big match coming up. She practices all the time so she can keep up her muscle memory. It's the same way with your voice. You just keep getting better and smoother the more you work on it.

Finding the right vocal coach is often a word-of-mouth affair; the best ones don't often need to advertise and may not take on everyone who calls. It really is okay to ask people you admire who they work with; I've even answered fan letters at the theatre that ask questions like this. I'm always happy to take a few minutes to help mentor an up-and-comer and give recommendations when I can. If you have no one to ask personally, you can also go online on sites like Broadway World.com and ask for recommendations on their forum.

Like many other things, you need to find the person who's the right fit for you. The coach I love might not be the right one for someone else; it's a matter of personality and style, and it's okay to try several coaches if you haven't found one you click with yet. Good coaches aren't cheap, but they can make the difference between you having a short career or a long one; you don't want to find yourself losing your voice ten years down the line because you fried it with improper technique on your first professional shows.

In New York, I also recommend taking workshops at One On One (OneonOneNYC.com). My own agency and casting directors I know teach classes there. You may do monologues or scene studies, and the cool part is that they put you on camera and go over it with you to show you how you're performing, what strange things you might be doing without realizing it, and how you're improving.

For acting classes, word of mouth has been my best guide. One of the best classes I ever attended was based in someone's apartment. It's not always about the building but about the quality of the teacher.

For dance, the two studios I recommend most are Broadway Dance Center (www.broadwaydancecenter.com) and Steps on Broadway (www.stepsnyc.com). Both of them have many Broadway choreographers come in to teach master classes.

When you take classes from people who actually make casting decisions, it's a major bonus. It looks good for you to have the casting director or someone on the creative team recognize you and know that you're in class every week taking your craft seriously.

It's Never Too Late

Michael McCorry Rose got started in theatre in the same way that lots of boys do: There weren't enough boys trying out for the high school musical, so someone asked him if he'd do it.

"I said I knew what a musical was, which was better than most, I suppose."

He ended up being cast as Curly in *Oklahoma!* and loved the experience. Through the rest of high school and college, he continued acting, but it wasn't his focus. He was a mass communications major at UCLA because he wanted to do something in the entertainment field, but says, "I did not want to be a starving artist."

So he went into entertainment publicity—a field that enabled him to represent actors and actresses and be around the business without performing. Within a few years, though, he felt a "crisis of the soul" and realized he wasn't on the right path.

No one is going to create my life for me, he realized. *So what do I really want to do?*

At the age of twenty-five, he realized that he deeply wanted to perform, but fear was holding him back from pursuing it. He decided to change that. After taking voice lessons with a teacher from LA Opera twice a week for a year, Michael landed a role in a non-Equity tour of *Joseph and the Amazing Technicolor Dreamcoat,* traveling to different cities every couple of days.

He realized that to continue his career, he'd need to make up for lost time. "I had to make up for missing a four-year conservatory or university theatre experience, and that learning curve was steep and treacherous. I didn't know anything. I didn't know what a sixteen-bar cut meant, I didn't have a monologue, and when someone said, 'What's your technique?' I had no idea what they were asking."

He found that the theatre community was very supportive and that actors were more than willing to share information about acting classes they'd taken that helped them have breakthroughs. "It's a bit like adults going to night school after they've lived a little," he says, adding that continuing education is essential in this business. Ten years later, and after many professional credits, he continues taking classes.

A message he likes to share is that it's never too late. When he teaches now, parents often ask nervous questions about age—after all, many of us have heard that you'll never be a musical prodigy if you didn't start playing an instrument early in childhood. But there are lots of professional actors who either had never stepped on a stage or hadn't taken it seriously until well into adulthood.

Kathryn Joosten, who won two Emmys for her work as Mrs. McClusky on *Desperate Housewives,* didn't get started on an acting career until age forty-two. She had been a nurse and stay-at-home mom before a divorce left her in a position of starting over unexpectedly. She did some community theatre, working her way up to professional theatre, an Equity card, and an agent. But for twelve years she continued holding down other jobs because she wasn't supporting herself or her family through acting alone.

When her boys were grown, she took a job as a street performer at Disney, which finally convinced her that maybe she could make it as a full-time actress. Her biggest success came after she moved to Los Angeles and began landing television roles, one after another, on shows like *Frasier, Grey's Anatomy, Scrubs,* and *The West Wing.* So before her death at age seventy-two, she had acted for thirty years and worked at it full-time for eighteen years—no small feat.

It's more unusual for someone to find Broadway success if they haven't started working in their twenties, but the good news is that even though there are fewer roles for women over thirty and men over forty on Broadway, there's also less competition; people do drop out and move on to other things.

If it's what you love to do, it's never too late to give yourself that shot. You just have to be willing to put in the work to catch up.

Headshots

If you're eighteen or older, you do need professional headshots, not just a nice snapshot. You'll want to get a range of looks out of your shoot so that your agent or you can choose between them depending on what role you're going out for. At minimum, make sure you have one with a full-teeth smile and one serious. My agency has copies of three different headshots they can choose from.

There's a wide range of acceptable pricing for headshots. I know actors who do photography on the side and charge $200–$600 for headshots, and professionals who charge up to $5,000. You don't have to go anywhere near the upper range to get a good, workable headshot, though—just pay attention to the person's portfolio before you book. Make sure you're looking at their headshots, not event photos or other types of shots. Compare apples to apples. You need someone who understands what acting headshots are all about—they're not overly touched-up glamour shots or artistic modeling shots. They're you. The real you, with only minor fixes to remove stray hairs, zap a pimple, soften a shadow . . . things like that. It doesn't help you to arrive in a room and have the creative team frustrated because your photo looks like a supermodel instead of who you really are. Luckily, stage acting doesn't require you to be a supermodel. People are viewing you from a distance, with plenty of makeup on, and you don't need to be feature-perfect. No one's going to notice if you have a slightly chipped tooth or thin lips. Of course, if you have something about your appearance that you worry will hold you back (like, say, a *missing* tooth or a mole on your face), try to get it fixed before the headshots. If these are a specific part of your trademark look, of course, keep it.

Also pay attention to whether the photographers do shoots indoors or outdoors and what you prefer. Some photographers like to work with natural lighting, others with studio lighting. Either is okay.

Whenever you change your look (a big haircut, significant weight loss, and so on), you have to update your headshot, and of course, your headshot from age twenty is not still going to work for you when you're twenty-eight. So factor this in to your business expenses; it's an important part of your marketing tools.

Résumés

You don't need a professional to help you with your résumé unless you want someone to check for typos; the formatting is pretty simple, and you can look at examples online to set you on the right path. Here's Michael McCorry Rose's: www.michaelmccorryrose.com/about.

As you can see, it includes the following elements:

- Memberships (AEA, SAG, and so on).

- Height, hair color, weight, and eye color (you don't specify your age unless you're under eighteen—let them decide how old you look; you don't want to limit yourself).

- Credits in whatever areas you have credits—musical theatre, film, television, voiceovers, commercials, and so on.

- Training: Include relevant details about voice, acting, and dance training—who your teachers were and where you took classes, and how long you studied if that's relevant (for dance).

- Special skills: Anything that might be useful on stage. Don't bother with things that can't be seen, like "good at math" or "trained as a photographer." Specific accents you can do and languages you speak, impersonations you can do, gymnastics/acrobatic skills, instruments you play, athletic skills, baton twirling . . . things like that all belong in that section.

- Contact information: Your agent's or yours. At minimum, provide a phone number and email address.

When you're new to the business, the credit section is probably the most daunting, but a casting director advises that they expect you to have few significant credits if you're in your early twenties or under. You can put high school and college shows and community theatre on your résumé if that's all you have, though he advises not to write, for example, "Deerfield High School," and instead just write "Deerfield Theatre," along with the director's name. Just don't get carried away trying to write down every church and library play you ever did . . . pick the ones where you had lead roles or that show the kind of roles you're best at.

Why Not to Have a Fallback Career

I know it seems counterintuitive. Especially when you're in high school or college, nearly every adult will advise you to have a fallback career in case this acting thing doesn't work out. I say no.

Here's the simple reason why: When you have a fallback career, you're probably going to do the fallback career.

I mean, you spend all this time preparing for it. Having a fallback career means taking a lot of classes or doing training in an area that isn't related to your actual dream job. Then, when adversity strikes, you're most likely to think, *Well, this is why I trained in that fallback career. I'd better do that now.* And once you're started on that path, how will you get back to performing again? You can't be in a normal nine-to-five job and still go on auditions regularly. You can't up and leave your "other" career to do a show and then expect to be welcomed back to it. You can't work your way up the ladder in an office job while only halfway committed to it and ready to bail as soon as your big break comes through.

I believe that to make it as a performer, you have to be completely committed to it—no backup plans. Just you and your dream, figuring out a way to make it work.

Now, that doesn't mean you won't need to do things to make money outside of just the exact types of performing work you want to do. You definitely may need another job of some sort while waiting for acting gigs to come through, but it should be the kind of work that can be very flexible— weeknights after your auditions, or the ability to trade shifts with other people, or work-from-home jobs where you can make your own schedule. Waiting tables is the cliché, but there are other jobs that dovetail pretty well with an actor's life—things like catering, bartending, web design, and temp agency work. Some actors will tell you that it's best to come to New York with some restaurant experience so that you'll have a way to support yourself until your career is in full swing.

Personally, I tried to always work jobs that bore some relevance to my career. That would mean singing for weddings or bar and bat mitzvahs sometimes. It could also mean working backstage jobs—stage crew, set design, costumes, makeup . . . lots of people are needed to help shows run smoothly, and this can keep you connected to the theatre world even when you're not the one on stage. (I'm not suggesting you join the stagehands' union and go pro on this—just picking up occasional work in community and regional theatres.) Or you might be great at impersonations and do an act in an impersonators' show, or work as a backup dancer or singer for songwriter demos. I grew up in a dance studio, so teaching dance and singing is something I love. There are so many nooks and crannies of this business that you can find with a little work. I think it's important to keep fresh even when you're not actively in a show.

The simple truth is that it's very hard to make a living long term, especially one that will support your expenses in a city like New York, exclusively from musical theatre. It's a sobering fact that is responsible for why the herds get thinned— there are *lots* of people trying to become actors right after high school or college, and far fewer still out there in their forties and fifties, mostly because it can be frustrating to watch your peers pass you by financially. They're out there buying houses and cars and building their nest eggs, and you're just trying to afford groceries because your last gig ended four months ago and you haven't been cast again since then.

I have friends who've crossed over into other areas of the business (stage managing, directing, casting, and so on). But you *can* make a living just through performing as long as you diversify and keep busy even when you're not in a show.

Donna Vivino also looks for ways to make her own opportunities. When an arts center director from North Dakota reached out and told her he was a fan of hers, she directed the conversation toward work:

"I've always wanted to go to North Dakota. If you have a budget for solo concerts, let me know."

"Actually, we do. Would you want to come out?"

"Sure, if you fly me out and we negotiate a price."

She doesn't have an agent who handles concerts, so she was able to negotiate directly with him and flew out to do a few shows for them. She also reaches out to universities to offer her services teaching master classes when she's not booked up. But one of the boldest moves she made came on the heels of some backstage talk at *Hairspray*. A fellow actress expressed her disappointment that her agent hadn't gotten her an appointment to audition for *Martin Short: Fame Becomes Me.* The actress said they were looking for a replacement who was a great singer and good at comedic impressions, and Donna thought, *That's me. Why didn't I hear about this?*

She could have just sighed and let it go, but she felt strongly enough about it that she tried to figure out a way in, even knowing that the auditions had already taken place. She emailed the composer of *Hairspray,* who was also working on *Martin Short,* and explained her plight.

"I'm not sure if you know who I am, but I'm a chorus girl in your show. I heard about the call for a replacement in *Martin Short,* and I don't know if you've cast her yet, but it feels like something I could do. I'm an impersonator. Is there any chance I could audition?"

He wrote back, "This email reminds me of when I called Bette Midler from a pay phone and said, 'I know you use Barry Manilow all the time, but when he's not around, please give me a chance.' [They've been working together ever since.] The final callbacks are on Monday. We have people coming in from all over, but I want you to come in."

Taking that chance—which won't always work, of course—enabled her to skip the line and go to the final callback and book the job.

I'M WITH THE BAND

Call up entertainment companies and tell them you're available—many companies put together temporary bands on request as gigs come up, which means they call around to ask who's available from their roster of singers and musicians for a particular gig—usually weekends at night. It's not a long-term commitment, but it's something that keeps you in practice and gives you more performance experience. Plus you may mingle with more people in the business this way, and you never know where those connections lead.

My brand also includes teaching (I teach master classes and seminars all over the country) and a handbag and cosmetic line called FullBeat (www.fullbeat.com) specifically meant for performers who need to tote around lots of makeup, hair products, deodorant, and so on and want to do it with style. Everything I do has some connection to the acting world, even at times when acting itself is not bringing in the bulk of my income.

I want everything I do to reflect who I am, and the handbags and cosmetics fit in well with the girly image I want the world to see of me.

The Symphonic World

If you're a classically trained singer, make sure your agent and casting directors know if you're interested in doing work with symphonies.

Not all of it is opera; symphonies have some crossover with other styles, particularly musical theatre, because they may do shows devoted to Broadway where they're looking for singers with that sort of background. However, Ernest Richardson, the principal conductor for Omaha Symphony and the music director and principal conductor for Steamboat Symphony Orchestra, says that even for shows like that, they still usually lean toward wanting a classical sound.

"I hate the term *legit* because it implies that other sounds are not legit," he says, but that's another way people describe it. What he says he's looking for are singers who sing in a healthy manner. "Properly classically trained singers can sing in a healthy way in any style that's reasonable for their voice. I'm looking for the beauty of the human voice."

Another key quality he's looking for is versatility. "In our Christmas show, one minute our singers are doing a cinematic version of a Christmas carol, another minute they're doing tight harmonies in a Manhattan Transfer sort of style, and another, maybe they're doing a cover of a Michael Bublé song, going back and forth between all these styles."

Normally, there are just one to three rehearsals before you perform, so you have to have your material down cold before you get there. The rehearsals aren't for teaching you the music but about how to blend with the orchestra and other singers, how to stage it, and how to present you in your best light. Unlike musical theatre, where there's usually a large cast splitting the singing, in a symphony, there are just a few singers who need to be able to sing for hours.

Ernest uses a casting director to send singers his way. He doesn't do big open calls, so it's important to have your training on your résumé so that casting directors become familiar with what you can do.

Auditioning for a symphony is different from auditioning for a show because there's no character you have to portray. That can be really freeing if you're confident in your own stage persona, or intimidating if you like the safety net of having a role to fit into.

"A lot of the time, I find that singers enter the room trying to figure out what the people on the other side of the table want them to do, and that's not a good strategy. If a person can reveal who they are as a singer and actor, that's the most important thing. It's partly a maturation process.

Young singers are so busy figuring out how to fit in someone else's mold when they really need to search for who they are and how they can connect to an audience."

Symphony performing has minimal choreography—most of it is just standing there and singing—so it's important for you to not rely on someone giving you particular blocking or movements. You do what you do and focus on making a connection with the audience.

Don't Typecast Yourself

Sometimes I notice students gravitating toward certain roles not because those are their favorites but because someone once cast them that way. If the first director you ever worked with saw you as a Sandy from *Grease* type, you might just go along with the belief that those are the types of roles you should try out for. But you also might be selling yourself short.

Don't be afraid to experiment. Try out different monologues and types of songs to see if you have other strengths, too. I had to push back against the professors who thought I should be "edgier" so that I could find the roles that really fit me. And comedians like Robin Williams could get stuck always being "the funny guy," or they could have breakout dramatic roles like he did in *Good Will Hunting*. Some of the best dramatic actors started in comedy, where you have to get masterful at timing.

If you're trying to break out of a typecasting rut, you might want to aim for less competitive auditions where you'll have a chance to boost your résumé with roles that are more diverse—workshops, student films, regional theatre, and so on—so that you can show a director you're not just Sandy from *Grease*; you're also Rizzo. (Who knew?)

You don't want to fill your résumé with all small stuff, but it's good to show a range of roles, even if that means it's not all "big" shows.

Make Your Own Opportunities

I've mentioned before that even if you have an agent, manager, or both, you're still going to be your best representative. There were so many times earlier in my career when casting directors intimidated me; I thought I should leave the contacts up to my agent and just show up when they told me to.

Now I wish I'd realized sooner that you really can call or email a casting director yourself. They don't want you tying up their phones to give you career advice, but once you've met a casting director a couple of times, it's okay to call up to offer your services as a reader, or ask about an upcoming project, or invite them to come see a show of yours. Casting directors do like to see talent in their "natural habitat" (performing), not just auditioning, because they realize that some people are way better at performing in front of a full audience than they are in a small audition room.

Keep yourself in their minds as much as you can. Let them know you're ready to work and that you're not giving up. Although there's always new blood coming into the industry, the pool of regulars gets smaller and smaller as people move on, move out, or take breaks. Show them you're in it for the long haul.

11

Union or Nonunion?

It may seem obvious that you would want to be in the Actors' Equity Association (AEA) as quickly as you can if you want a theatrical performing career. After all, it raises the bar—you can get into auditions for professional shows that non-Equity talent can't. You get priority at open auditions. You get covered by the union's negotiating power to ensure fair pay and fair working conditions. And, even cooler, you get to carry around a card that's also carried around by the biggest Broadway stars, marking you as *one of their club*. It feels like a status symbol, like being guest-listed at an exclusive nightclub.

But.

There is a major downside to joining the union too quickly: It can be very limiting. You lose other opportunities that may be more your speed in the beginning. Once you're a union actor, you can't do non-Equity shows. You can't sign with a non-Equity-franchised talent agent. You can't even do favors for friends, like going back to the community theatre where you had so much fun and making a guest appearance in their holiday show. Even benefit shows need authorization from the Theatre Authority, a nonprofit associated with Actors' Equity and its sister unions. And all of that may sound like an acceptable trade-off until you can't find Equity work. You're basically trading opening the door to the highest-level work for closing and locking the door to lots of other work.

Here's the situation I ran into and which has been echoed by many of my acting friends:

I did my first Equity show in a regional theatre soon after college. I had the option of joining the union because of that show. There are three ways you get union membership—you are hired to perform under an Equity contract (and in some cases, you have to work a certain number of weeks before you're eligible), you have membership in a sister organization like SAG-AFTRA, or you work as an actor or stage manager at an Equity theatre (even if you don't have an Equity contract) for twenty-five weeks after you've applied for an Equity Membership Candidate Program.

I didn't *have* to join, but I could, as long as I applied and put down $400 toward my initiation fee during the run of the show—so I did! It meant, among other things, that I would now have good health insurance and workers' compensation protection, and I figured it would be a golden ticket that would enable me to get seen at lots of auditions and taken seriously. At the time, I could imagine only positives; I couldn't see any reason not to join.

But here's the truth: After that show, I got that huge string of rejections all over town. It was very difficult for me to get seen for appointments for auditions even with my Equity card. There are fifty thousand members, so even though it feels like an exclusive club, it's a pretty huge one! I was often waiting around at open calls, and I had so little professional experience and no name recognition back then, which made it easy for casting directors to overlook me in favor of people they were already familiar with who had much stronger résumés.

So in the interim, I wasn't performing.

It was painful not to perform! In the past, I was in college shows, regional theatre, summer stock . . . whatever I wanted to do, I could do. Now I was not allowed, and yet I couldn't get the work I *was* allowed to do. The only thing that kept me in the theatre world was taking classes; I continued to study and go to workshops, and I continued going to any audition that sounded remotely like a fit for me, whether for an ensemble or principal role. It's not that I was being picky; I just got a very fast, hard crash to reality during that time that made me realize just how competitive professional theatre is. I just wanted to be on stage; it didn't matter if I was in the way back of the stage in a costume that made me unrecognizable—just let me get out there! Alas, nothing came for a good long time.

I had already paid my fees to join the union, which is no small figure; as of 2018, there's a $1,600 initiation fee due within the first two years that goes toward administrative costs, plus $170 a year for basic dues (payable half in May, half in November), plus 2.375 percent of all your gross earnings up to $300,000 a year (deducted automatically from weekly payroll and scheduled to go up to 2.5 percent in 2019). Basically, I was still paying off my initiation fee, but my weekly paycheck had already dried up. I felt like I was paying to be handcuffed, and I started resenting it.

I resented it again when I was asked to set *The Drowsy Chaperone* tour and had to argue and get special permission because it was non-Equity. Even though I was not performing, they still didn't want my name associated with a non-Equity show. The director had to write a letter to convince them that this was a good opportunity for me and wouldn't harm them.

You may think you're ready to jump into that bigger pond with union actors, but the truth is that it can be truly difficult to go from having lots of lead roles in school and local shows to auditioning all over New York and not even making callbacks. It can also be confusing when you think you've learned all you need to know *because* of those lead roles; sometimes people think that because they were one of the best in their school, that means they're done learning and ready to go pro. Even after going to a performing arts high school and a conservatory and having a mom who owned a dance studio, though, I wasn't done learning in my early twenties. I'm still not done learning today.

Actors' Equity rarely lets people take breaks, either. Sometimes they'll let children take a break to do a school show, but an adult in my situation has little hope: I couldn't put my membership on hold for a while so that I could do some non-union shows and build up my résumé and keep performing. And although you can ask to be put on "inactive status" with the union so that you won't have to pay dues for a while, you *still* can't do non-Equity shows while you're listed as inactive.

That's why I kept my membership even when I shifted gears and began teaching and doing symphony concerts as my main income (which are not a conflict with the union)—I spent about two years without doing an Equity show, yet I still had to pay my dues or start all over again. This is one of those strange industries where you don't actually have to be actively working in your field to remain qualified; you just have to qualify once and then pay indefinitely. There are so many people who get their Equity card and then don't get cast for years and years. At any given time, far fewer than half of all Equity members are actually employed in Equity shows.

When an actor friend moved out of state, he found that there was no Equity theatre nearby, so he asked Equity to allow him to take a break. They refused, so he ended up giving up his membership. Equity's position is that if you quit, it's forever. To be reinstated—which is rarely granted—you have to go in front of the board and plead your case, but quitting so you can work nonunion jobs is not a valid reason. If they do allow you to rejoin, you have to requalify and pay a new initiation fee.

This is why I suggest that most actors hold off on joining Equity until they have to, even if that sounds counterintuitive.

First, unless you're going to live in New York or Los Angeles, the trade-off probably isn't worth it. It limits what you can do regionally and doesn't offer the same benefits of getting you into the local auditions. There are working professional actors outside of the major markets who've been non-Equity their entire careers because they'd rather perform consistently at lower-paying jobs than wait around to get an occasional high-paying gig.

And even if you do live in a major market, a young actor needs performing experience, and most of the time that will come in the form of non-Equity shows.

You don't always have a choice about joining. You may be able to get an audition and get hired for a Broadway show without an Equity card, but you have to join the union before you can start performing. That's the agreement Broadway theatres have with the union—all of its actors must be Equity. But other theatres have different agreements, where only a certain percentage of their actors must be Equity. There are at least thirty different Equity contracts that cover all kinds of performance situations and theatre sizes. I'm doing a regional theatre show right now where they're able to hire just two or three Equity actors—and I'm one of those actors!

Rotating Doors

Another issue is that some theatres that were Equity are no longer so, or tours that were originally Equity may close and send out non-Equity versions. And, of course, vice versa: Equity noticed that too many tours were going out as non-Equity, so they created new contracts to encourage tour producers to stick with the union.

Every now and then, a producer chooses not to go Equity for other reasons, but it's normally a financial decision. It's just more expensive to go Equity, including actors' salaries, health insurance, pensions, per diems, overtime, travel, and so on. It especially hits smaller theatres hard.

"Smaller experimental theatres in LA weren't able to have

Equity contracts because they had, say, seventy seats, and a good night for them was forty tickets sold. They can't afford to pay actors $800 a week," says regional theatre director Bobby Logue. "So there was a 99 Seat Plan that allowed them to just pay small stipends, and Equity took it away, so many of those theatres closed."

It was a big controversy because members had voted to leave the old ninety-nine-seat plan in place, but Equity chose not to. They enacted a new plan that required those theatres to pay at least minimum wage to actors, and even that was impossible for many. While Equity declared it a win, it meant again shrinking the pool of places where union actors are allowed to perform.

EPA and ECC Calls

If you check out *Backstage,* you'll frequently see listings for EPA (Equity Principal Audition) and ECC (Equity Chorus Call). When you're new to this, they look really exciting: *Wow!* Dear Evan Hansen *has a call for new principal actors? I'm there!*

The thing is, the union requires all shows with Equity Production Agreements (the highest level—which includes Broadway, national and international tours from Broadway, and several top-tier regional theatres and performing arts centers) to hold these Equity open calls every six months— even if they're *not* looking for any new talent. So it can look deceiving; you may show up for this audition thinking they're ready to replace the lead actor, but they have no intention of doing so and already have three other actors lined up for when their lead signs off or they already have the actors they're seriously considering scheduled to audition through agent appointments.

They're also not allowed to hold auditions by appointment for any new shows until they've had their initial EPA and ECC. They may have a whole slate of actors they expect to hire through appointments, but they're not able to announce a cast until they do those EPAs and ECCs first, making it something of a formality.

That doesn't mean it's not worth going; it just means it may not fit your original expectations.

Given the choice between going to the chorus call or the principal call, most actors hope to land a spot in the principal call for obvious reasons, but either one can work for you. You don't have to choose; you can go to both. You're more likely to be seen at an ECC as a non-Equity actor.

At EPAs, when you're singing, you will (according to union rules) get to sing a minimum of thirty-two bars of a song. The breakdown should have information about what to prepare in terms of monologues or songs. Your audition is expected to last for about two minutes.

Equity actors now sign up online for EPA slots; as of this writing, two-thirds of all slots are available via the member portal at noon one week before the audition day. The other third of the slots are available for Equity actors who show up in person the morning of the audition. You sign up for a twenty-minute slot, and unlike at doctors' offices, they guarantee to see you within those twenty minutes, so you won't have to wait around all day wondering how late they're running—which does happen with agent appointments. Sometimes when you have an agent appointment that's not part of an EPA, you can find yourself sitting around an hour later still waiting to be called.

At EPAs, they schedule six auditions for every twenty-minute time slot. If anyone doesn't show up, or if they're running ahead of schedule, they also have "alternate" lists of Equity members who either didn't get a time slot or who are waiting around hoping to be seen earlier than their assigned time.

If there is time left after alternates are seen, and if the producers decide to, non-Equity actors will also be seen in their order of arrival, with Equity member candidates (EMC) getting priority. EMCs are actors who are working or have worked at an Equity theatre and have paid a registration fee but haven't yet accrued enough work weeks to be full-fledged members or have chosen not to join quite yet. As of 2018, you need at least twenty-five weeks of Equity work for full membership, but you can postpone membership until you've reached fifty weeks—otherwise you forfeit your registration fee and credits. You may remain an EMC for years.

Depending on the popularity of the show, it does happen that not all slots will be taken, or that several Equity actors won't show, or that auditions will run quicker than anticipated and there will be time for non-Equity actors. But it's a different game that requires a lot more sitting around and a lot more potential for wasted time.

Often, non-Equity actors will show up in the wee hours of the morning in front of an audition studio and start their own unofficial list. This is done on the honor system and may or may not be respected by the monitor, who arrives one hour prior to the scheduled call. Let's say Joe goes to the theatre and puts his name on the list at 5:00 a.m. He's number ten on the list at that time. Then he goes back to his apartment to take a nap. When he returns after the monitor has arrived, there's a good chance he'll still be number ten on the non-Equity list when that list becomes official—but there's also a chance that the monitor will refuse to honor any lists made before he or she arrived.

Another possible ugly thing that happens is that other actors may take and change the lists before the monitor arrives, switching around the order to add themselves earlier, or leaving out several people. There's not much you can do about this; the only way to protect yourself is to stay on that line the entire time. Even so, the monitor won't sort it out if someone "cuts" you on line, like when one person is holding places for her four roommates. And monitors are actors themselves who are sometimes hoping to get an audition spot, too, which I've always thought is a conflict of interest!

Unofficial lists aren't accepted at the Actors' Equity Association (AEA) Audition Center, which is one of the main audition studios. They put up their official non-Equity sign-up sheets when the building opens (currently 6:30 a.m.). Non-Equity actors aren't allowed to go past the second-floor lobby, which means you can't even use the bathroom in the building; you have to go across the street, so don't wait until shortly before your number may be called.

Even though it's admirable that some people show up at 4:00 or 5:00 a.m. to wait on line, my casting director friend thinks it's a bad idea. "How well are you going to perform when you haven't slept?" So get there early, but not *that* early!

You can find out at the monitor's desk who's in the room—which casting people will be on the other side of the desk. If you're not familiar with the names, it's a good idea to look them up and learn what you can about their backgrounds. It can be disappointing to find out that you're auditioning for an assistant at a casting agency, which does happen, but it's still always smart to make connections and good impressions as often as you can.

ECCs are similar to EPAs, but with some benefits for non-Equity actors: There are no Equity alternates, and EMCs don't get special priority, so you have a better shot of making it into the room if appointments run fast or people don't show. And the rules say that at least one member of the creative team has to be in the room, as opposed to EPAs where you may see an assistant.

Often, once auditions get under way, they will dismiss non-Equity people until after the lunch break as long as it's clear they won't get through the appointments and alternates before then. Sometimes they announce right away that they won't be seeing any non-Equity people but that they'll accept drop-offs (your headshot and résumé). It's worth it to leave yours—there really are people who've been called for an appointment and cast based on these drop-offs. And sometimes you'll show up bright and early and find out hours later that they won't see any non-Equity people *and* won't take drop-offs. Those are the breaks.

Equity members must be there at ECC calls half an hour before your time slot, because the monitor will call your number half an hour early—and if you're not there, you get crossed off the list. You may get another shot after everyone else goes, or you may not, depending on timing.

The chorus calls are either for singers or dancers, but be prepared for both—bring your dance shoes *and* your book because sometimes they'll ask you to stay for a second audition on the spot.

As you move further along in your career, you'll rely less on these EPAs and ECCs and be able to book more appointments, though higher-level actors do still attend them sometimes when it's a show they really love and they didn't get an appointment or it's a creative team they really want to impress.

"It's a numbers game, and you want to get as many at-bats as possible to get a good average," says Michael McCorry Rose. "If you're waiting around only for appointments, it's hard to get enough at-bats."

Especially in the beginning, it's smart to get experience auditioning any way you can. Not only are you possibly making connections, but you're gaining experience and learning how to get through the process so you don't feel like your whole life is riding on each audition.

AUDITION UPDATE

You can monitor the progress of an audition by following www.auditionupdate.com (run by *Backstage*). It's a series of message boards where you can read and post firsthand reports about auditions; you'll often see notes there about who's in the room, how many people are signed up, where they are in the alternates list once auditions are under way, and whether or not they're seeing nonunion actors. It can save you a trip or encourage you to hurry over to an audition you weren't sure about. There's also a board there to compare notes about callbacks and an often-hilarious "Bitching Post," where people write about things that have gone horribly wrong—like a recent post in which someone complained about being fired from an Equity job for destroying a backstage toilet with a cherry bomb. Joke or serious post? You decide.

Union Benefits

Although I can't say everything about the union is rosy (it can often feel cold and impersonal, in addition to the restrictions), I do want to acknowledge that they work to protect actors' rights and ensure we'll be treated fairly in terms of things like housing, travel, extra pay for extra work, and so on.

While many nonunion theatres are great, there are also horror stories about conditions in nonunion shows. One theatre had literal holes in the stage dropping all the way down to the basement, so part of the choreography was directing the dancers to jump around the holes. Other theatres have insisted on rehearsals well into the night, or no days off, or bug-infested living quarters (and, of course, frequently really bad pay). Some will make you pay for your own costumes or particular tap shoes even though they cost more than your weekly pay. The union is very good about making sure conditions are safe, sanitary, and fair for members, with established breaks and time off, and that your show-related expenses are covered. If you happen to have those particular tap shoes, for instance, then Equity requires the producers to "rent" them from you—essentially paying you a small amount of extra money to account for wear and tear on your property.

Union rules and contracts are forever changing and being renegotiated, so it would be impossible to give a full breakdown in a book (it would be outdated by its publication date), but just understand that there are many different levels and types of union contracts, certainly not all with the same terms. Some companies will fly you from place to place; others will put you on a bus. There may be different minimum amounts of time before they have to cover your health insurance, different per diems when traveling, different housing requirements.

The top tier is the Production Agreement (Broadway, first national and international tours, and so on); the lower-level touring agreement is the Short Engagement Touring Agreement (SETA), which has six categories; and most regional theatres use the League of Resident Theatres (LORT) Agreement, which has different minimum salary requirements based on their average weekly gross box office receipts. Currently, there are seventy-two member theatres around the country operating under LORT. There are also much more specific and limited agreements such as the Dinner Theatre Agreement, the Buffalo/Rochester Agreement, the Hollywood Area Theatre Agreement, and the Casino Agreement. Each one aims to provide safe and sanitary working conditions, minimum salary requirements that include provisions for overtime and extra work, required auditions, pensions and health benefits (not all agreements provide for this), supplemental workers' compensation, and bonding protection.

The minimum salaries are just that—minimums. Your agent (or you) can always try to negotiate for more, but the union does provide a floor. If the pay is below a certain point on tiered and SETA contracts, you also get a percentage of the show's profits (if it makes any), known as *overages*.

But with these new tiered touring contracts, some union jobs actually pay less than some nonunion regional theatres, which makes the distinction feel meaningless. Just because it's a union contract doesn't mean it's high paying. Equity actors often have to turn down touring jobs because they can't justify leaving their families behind or leaving the other job opportunities in New York for such a meager salary.

You have to work at least eleven weeks per year to get your health insurance covered for six months, or nineteen weeks per year to have it covered year-round. If you have less than that, then you can buy into their health plans, which have been very good plans in my experience.

The union has been around since 1913, and without it, it's very likely that conditions for actors would be much worse. Before the union, it was a lot easier for producers to get away with not paying for rehearsals or travel expenses, not providing benefits, not giving actors adequate breaks, and so on. Some have even acknowledged that they would never have improved terms for actors if the union hadn't forced them to. I very much appreciate the backbone of the union even if I don't agree with all its rules.

12

Tips from a Casting Director

Casting directors (CDs for short) see actors all day at auditions, and often all night at performances, so they know a lot about how we operate! They understand how hard it is to make it in this business, and they get that every one of us just wants to impress them. But there are smart ways to do that . . . and not-so-smart ways.

Social Media

Cesar Rocha (who's also my friend on social media, I should add—but only became so after we'd met each other numerous times and worked together) mentions how awkward it feels for him when performers try to connect with him on social media.

His Facebook account isn't a professional one, it's personal. It has pictures of his nieces and nephews and stories about what he bought his best friend for his birthday, not notes about theatre. So it feels invasive when actors he doesn't know well send him friend requests. Right now, he has a few hundred friend requests languishing because he doesn't feel comfortable letting every actor in town into his personal life.

"If someone has public accounts—like my Instagram and Twitter accounts are both public—then feel free to follow and comment. But it crosses a boundary when you're trying to get access to private content."

Email vs. Snail Mail

Each casting director may have slightly different preferences, but my friend offers a few suggestions: First, he says that all snail mail crosses his desk, and he does open everything and look at it. He prefers seeing headshots and résumés this way, and he likes that he's not pressured to hit Reply.

Email is fine, too, if the casting director has given out an email address, but don't send big attachments. He says that if something comes in larger than 2 MB, he deletes it unread if it's not from someone he knows, because his email account has limited space. So don't send huge headshot files. Don't get annoyed if he doesn't reply unless he requested that you email him something; casting directors are inundated with email all day long and rarely respond unless it's to express immediate interest.

Cesar *doesn't* give out his email address publicly but says that it's usually pretty easy to figure out an agency's email formula. When you're coming in with a referral from someone he knows, he doesn't mind an email, but he says that contacts out of the blue feel like when you get a call from an unknown number—*How did they find me?* He prefers that people stick to publicly available contact information until they have a relationship with him and he offers more.

Even then, he says, some people like to reach out by email every couple of weeks without any particular reason. He understands they're trying to stay fresh in his mind, but he says that it's overkill.

"Definitely write to me when you have something to say—like if you have new headshots, new representation, or you just landed your first Broadway show. Don't write to tell me you got good feedback at an open call."

A big pet peeve of his is that several actors have added him to their email mailing lists without his approval. This means that they send him mass mailings about their latest shows and appearances, which makes him think badly of them. If he didn't ask to be on a mailing list, he doesn't want to be on it!

Invitations to Shows

Do write or call to invite casting directors to see you in your performances, though, with a few caveats.

"There was a woman who used to write to me about every little thing she did," Cesar says. "She would say, 'I'm in a production, and it's a spaghetti dinner in my church basement, and tickets are twenty dollars.' You're trying to create a professional relationship with someone who casts Broadway shows, and you have to portray the image that you're ready for that. Pick and choose what you invite casting directors to, because if you don't think it's going to show you off as a professional person who can do the work, it's not worth it."

Not only is he highly unlikely to show up to those types of performances, but it also creates the idea in his mind that that's your level. You don't want to be the "spaghetti dinner" actor. Wait until you have something bigger.

Then, he much prefers it when emails have a personal touch. Mention his latest project. Say you hope casting is going well on the show you know he's working on, or anything else that shows you know who he is and that you respect him, not that you're just blanket-submitting invitations to everyone in the business and hoping someone will show up.

Make sure his ticket is comped, too, and if there's a drink minimum, cover it. You're asking a favor—you want this person to spend his or her free time watching you perform in hopes that it'll help you get a job—so you need to cover the cost. You can ask your director if the seat can be comped; they're often happy to know that industry professionals are in the audience. If not, then pay for the seat yourself once you have a confirmation.

Understand that the casting director may leave early, and that may not mean anything bad. They may have other commitments or may have seen all they needed to. Sometimes they're even trying to fit in more than one show per night.

Let's Hang Out

The overly friendly approaches don't work for Cesar or most other casting directors, either. Friendships should form naturally over time and after a good amount of conversation. Trying to butter up industry professionals by inviting them to hang out with you doesn't feel genuine.

Cesar tells a story about an actress who emailed him with what, at first, appeared to be a personal letter of gratitude. In it, she said that he was one of the people who inspired her to keep going in her career and that she was grateful that he was always a champion for her in the room. Then she invited him out to dinner so that she could "talk about the business" and ask for his career advice.

He stared at this email and realized two things: He had no idea who she was, and it was a form letter that she had copied and pasted, which he figured out based on the telltale indented formatting. After doing some research, he figured out that he had seen her once or twice at an open call, but she wasn't someone he had any relationship with, and he sure wasn't about to spend his night at dinner giving free advice to someone he'd barely met who was sending that same letter to casting directors all over town. That's his personal time, and he can spend it either with his family and friends or on worthwhile professional pursuits (like seeing performances), but what he can't do is take up lots of time letting people pick his brain when they're new to the business. That's what classes, mentors, workshops, and actor friends are for.

"I love actors. I do . . . but I want to go home to my dog," he says.

Keep Skills Current

When you're filling out the skills section of your résumé, make sure it's realistic and current. Cesar says that multiple times, he's called someone in specifically because of a skill they listed on a résumé: that they know how to backflip or can play the violin, for instance. But then when he gets them in the room and asks them to perform, they say, "Oh, I'm rusty. I haven't done a backflip in a year," or "I haven't played violin since college."

When you list skills, understand that you can be asked to show them at any moment. You'll likely have twenty-four hours to prepare. So if it's something you're confident you can dust off and do again with just a couple of hours to refresh yourself, then go ahead and list it, but don't bother listing things you studied in high school if you can't confidently show that skill at an audition. It calls everything on your résumé into question when you show up and can't perform what you claimed you could.

That said, he does search for skills that specific! So if you *can* do a backflip, make sure it's in your skills section.

It's Okay to Be Green

Casting directors often talk about new talent as being *green*—not quite ready or experienced enough to take it to the next level. There's no shame in that. Everyone starts out that way. It doesn't mean you're untalented, just maybe not polished enough or confident enough, or maybe your credits don't yet show that you're capable of handling something bigger.

Cesar says that first impressions do matter and that many casting directors will remember an actor who made a strong impression in either direction, good or bad, so be careful about not showing up unprepared. Don't get seen by the A-list creative teams when you're not ready to be seen by the A-list creative teams. It could really harm you long term.

But then there are the ones who start out green and surprise him.

"I saw a girl at an audition for *Rent,* and I thought, *She's okay. Not knock my socks off.*" About eight months later, her agent called to say, "I know you saw her and said you felt like she needed work and wasn't ready. I just saw her in a new show off Broadway, and she was amazing. She has one ticket left; it's completely sold out, and she wants to give you the ticket. I think it would be worth it for you to go see her again. You can leave at intermission."

Although Cesar wasn't particularly optimistic, he trusted the agent enough to want to do her the favor, so he showed up—and he was blown away and happily stayed until the end. "I'm going to see her for everything," he decided.

That's what he says can happen when you take direction well and continue working on your craft. He says that when he gives feedback that someone isn't ready yet, he doesn't want to hear from them again two weeks later. There's no point arguing your case at that point; he's already formed an initial impression. But if you wait at least five or six months, he will be open to seeing you again.

And if you've seen a particular casting director numerous times without getting cast, that doesn't mean "no forever." It could just mean it just hasn't been the right match yet, or it could mean that he or she hasn't been blown away yet. But with more work, that could change.

"You're not the same actor today that you were two years ago," he says. "And you won't be the same actor in two years, either. You'll have new training, new shows under your belt, you'll have worked with choreographers who've choreographed Broadway shows and New York voice teachers who've helped you work on your belt. Keep showing up, because you never know."

Auditions and Agents

It's important to get yourself out there a lot—even more important than securing an agent, Cesar says.

"An agent may or may not get you in the room, but you're the one who still has to audition. The agent can't do that for you."

You have to gain the audition experience, so just keep going to open calls, EPAs, and ECCs, particularly for things that are attainable for newcomers.

A popular revival coming back to Broadway is likely to attract every seasoned Broadway actor around to its initial EPA, so if you're a non-Equity actor, it's probably not worth your time to wait on line for hours only to get turned away at the end. There's never going to be extra time to see non-Equity at a call like that. Even if you have your Equity card, the competition will be staggering. Instead, with EPAs and ECCs, focus on the big regional theatres that often transfer to Broadway, or long-running Broadway shows that need replacements, or tours, he says.

"Those are going to be the places you're going to be seen. I know Broadway is the goal, but I've seen plenty of people who work at the Muny with Chris Bailey or Kathleen Marshall or Dan Knechtges, and the next thing you know, they're going into Broadway auditions because they've worked with that person," he says. "The priority should be going to calls where there's a viable possibility you could get a job. Go to the Paper Mill. Go to the SETA contract tours. Go to the *Mean Girls* call if you're a young person—we cast a lot of those actors through the EPAs and ECCs."

The advice doesn't apply as much if you have a specialized skill they're looking for—like if you're a real, trained ballerina and they need ballerinas for *Carousel* on Broadway. Then go.

Or look for truly open calls. Once, when he was casting *Wicked,* he says there was a "drought" where he couldn't find suitable Elphaba understudies. He'd sent three people over, but the creative team didn't approve them, so he and another casting director held a big open call. They put out the word that they wanted everyone to just sing the ending of "The Wizard and I," because that's the hardest vocal part. Literally just a few bars. Anyone who did that well would get an appointment for a callback.

They went through 360 auditions that day in three hours, and one stood out most to him: Phoenix Best. She didn't wind up getting the job, but he thought she was just terrific, and he'd never seen her before. She was unagented and had no Broadway credits but was doing regional theatre. After a couple of callbacks, he called an agent friend of his and said, "There's this girl I just saw for Elphaba. She's fantastic, and you need to meet with her. I think you'd vibe with her."

The agent did sign her, and soon thereafter, she made her Broadway debut in *The Color Purple* and was just cast as a replacement in *Dear Evan Hansen*. That's the ideal situation: when you can impress someone so much in the room that they wind up being your best PR representative! If she hadn't stood in line along with hundreds of other young women to sing a few bars, her path to Broadway might not have come so quickly.

Small Talk

Don't worry if there's little to no conversation in the room. Sometimes a director will engage with you as soon as you enter ("I love those shoes! Where can I get a pair like that?"), and sometimes it's really just "Hi," and off you go. Some directors prefer to just sit in the back of the room quietly and listen, while others like to "direct" an audition.

Performers can try to read too much into the conversations, figuring that a lot of talk means they have a shot and no talk means the creative team didn't like them. Really, a lack of talk could mean the director has a headache, or they're in a hurry and just focused on the singing or dancing. There's no strong pattern to it—there have been times when I thought, *They talked to me so much. They must have loved me!* and then heard nothing, and times when I thought they weren't interested at all because it was such a quick in-and-out audition but I got a callback.

We all do it, but it's still a waste of time trying to over-analyze how it went. You have to try your best to leave the audition behind as soon as you exit the building.

Rooting for You

Remember that every casting director is rooting for you to be terrific. They all want to "discover" you and be able to recommend you for the part (or for other parts). When you walk into the room, they're hoping you're going to be The One just as much as you are. Always believe that they're on your side.

13

Child Actors

If you ask children what they want to be when they grow up, the number-one answer you'll hear is some kind of performer—singer or actor. The cool thing, too, is that kids have this innate self-confidence; they have no idea yet if they have any actual talent. They like to sing? Then they sing! They might be tone deaf, but they're still out there giving it their all on everything from "Happy Birthday" to Beyoncé songs. They're also *masters* of "dancing like nobody's watching," except that they often demand for everyone to watch.

Parents, then, have the sometimes challenging job of figuring out just how serious a child's dream is and how fervently to support it.

My friend Donna Vivino made it to Broadway when she

was eight years old. She lived in New Jersey, just twelve miles out of New York City, and had told her mother when she was five years old that she wanted to be an actress. *Now.* She'd grown up in a musical family (her dad is in Conan O'Brien's band), though not specifically a theatrical one.

She wanted to be on television and in movies like the ones she was watching on Nickelodeon. Seeing that her daughter had an outgoing personality and a flair for singing, her mother had Donna meet with a manager named Shirley in New Jersey. Shirley had her try to read a script for a commercial, which was tough for a kid who didn't solidly know how to read yet, and in the end, Shirley sent them home with a polite rejection. "It's all about blonde hair and blue eyes. She's not going to get anything right now. If she's still interested in a couple of years, try me again."

Donna had brown hair and brown eyes, and she wasn't enough of a standout actress to overcome what the manager saw as an "out of vogue" look. Donna's parents decided to let their daughter do what she could locally, so she tried out for *Annie* at a community theatre.

"I started singing, and they cut me off after the first line. I burst into tears," she remembers.

She didn't go on any other theatrical auditions, but two years later, Donna was still insistent that acting was what she wanted to do. Her mother took her for dance lessons and then brought her back and had her sing for Shirley. This time, they agreed to sign her and began sending her out on commercial auditions.

Donna booked several commercials and a CBS television show, and then came an opportunity to audition for *Les Misérables*.

"I don't want to go," she said. She was more interested in television and was still a bit traumatized from her last singing audition.

"You don't have to," her dad said.

"I think you should. Shirley says it's a really good musical, and a big one," her mom said—and in the end, Donna decided, *Fine*. She'd give it a shot.

She sang for the creative team and then didn't hear a word for seven months. They were auditioning kids all over the country. Finally, she heard back that she was invited to the callbacks. After several callbacks, she found out that she got the part. She would originate the role of Young Cosette (that's her on the original cast recording!).

Before Broadway, they did what's called an *out-of-town tryout*, meaning that they mounted the show in Washington, D.C., to gauge reactions before spending the money on a full Broadway production. Obviously it went well, because *Les Misérables* ended up being one of the longest-running shows in Broadway history.

There were just a few other kids in the show. She was the only local, which was just nice happenstance. One of the Gavroche boys moved from California, and Donna's understudy was from Alabama. Sometimes one parent goes with the child actor while the rest of the family stays home, and sometimes the whole family uproots to follow an opportunity like this.

Donna had a height restriction in her clause that said she could play the role until she had grown four inches. Luckily, she grew slowly and was able to play the role for two and a half years, until she was ten and a half.

Broadway for Kids

Donna was an exception to some of the challenges of "kid stardom" because she was able to live at home in New Jersey and continue going to her local school, for the most part. During the first four months in Washington, D.C., and during the rehearsals during the day in New York, she had to have a tutor, but she went back to her school after that time. She was able to do that because they didn't have Wednesday matinées, so all her performances were nights and weekends.

Her parents were determined that she would have a normal childhood aside from the show. They could have put her in a special school for performers, where she could miss time whenever she needed for jobs, but they didn't. They told her she had to keep up with her homework and her grades or they'd pull her from the show, and she's really happy about that now.

She's glad she wasn't comparing audition notes with her peers or living in a competitive world of stage moms. Backstage at *Les Misérables,* the kids goofed around and got in trouble like kids do. She still had her regular school and neighborhood friends to keep her grounded, she was a great student, and she wasn't treated like a big star. She never really realized what a big deal it was that she had a role on Broadway because it was treated as just part of her life and not her big meal ticket.

If you're an out-of-town family and your child gets cast, then there's a hurry to find local housing, which is rarely affordable. It's not something I often advise parents with school-age kids to do, because it's highly unsteady work at a time when kids need to focus on finishing their schooling and making sure this is even worth the sacrifices in their future lives. It also usually means just breaking even financially even if your child gets a major Broadway role because it means at least one parent or guardian needs to move to New York with the child . . . that means travel expenses, housing, local transportation, and so on for two people are riding on the child's salary—also taking into consideration that a portion of the money must be put into a trust for the child and can't be spent on those expenses. It also means splitting up the family more often than not—Dad and sister may stay home in Kentucky, while Mom and brother may be in New York. How will that play out long term?

"On tour, the company manager arranges housing, and you'll have maybe three options based on what you want to spend," says Nora Brennan of Nora Brennan Casting (who's cast children in the Broadway shows *Matilda the Musical, Billy Elliot the Musical,* and others). "In New York, you're on your own, and they don't pay expenses. It's a huge commitment."

She explains that most children's contracts are for six months with an option for another six months because kids grow and change so fast. If the child grows too tall, that's the end of the contract.

While you don't have to go to college (or technically even finish high school) to be an actor, Nora agrees that it's something all students should do if they're able. "Things change. You might get injured or be unable to perform. In school, you can also study lighting, sound, props, stage management, company management, casting . . . there are many opportunities in theatre besides performing."

She also says that children don't need agents to be cast on Broadway. "Every show has open calls every six months, and most of the kids we cast are from open calls."

Nora also advises parents not to push their kids into acting if they don't really, really love it—even if they're good at it, because "we can tell in five seconds if a kid isn't into it."

Chaperones

One of the things that surprises parents is that they can't stay with their kids during Broadway shows. They don't hang out backstage, and they don't get to watch the show unless they've bought a ticket. (You don't get a bunch of comps like you might in community theatre.) Instead, they have to drop their child off at the stage door and disappear. They can sometimes wait in the lobby if they have nowhere else to go, but the rule is that no parents or guardians come into the theatre with the child.

There are several reasons for this—insurance and liability issues are the easy one for directors to cite, but it's also about how the child is directed. Many kids do better without a parent there to "coach" them or judge their performance. The director wants to be the only one giving the child notes and wants the child to communicate directly with him or her. Plus it would be chaotic with many parents hanging around backstage. So instead there's a chaperone for the children whose job it is to keep them safe from drop-off time until the parent or guardian picks them up again.

There's a level of trust involved there, and you have to know your child will be okay going off without you for several hours at a time.

Gap Years

One of the challenges for child actors is that there are very few good parts for adolescents and teenagers both in theatre and film/TV. Historically, there've been lots of roles for young kids (think Annie, Oliver, Young Cosette and Gavroche in *Les Misérables,* Charlie in *Charlie and the Chocolate Factory,* and so on) and plenty of good roles for people in their twenties and up, but there's a strong gap in between. That's another reason to think twice about joining any of the unions as a child if you can avoid it; you're likely going to pay dues for several years when there just aren't any roles for you that pay professionally, and you won't be able to take other opportunities in the meantime.

Kids need that time to continue developing their skills and doing nonunion shows. School, community, and camp plays are the right training ground for most kids. Almost no one makes a seamless transition from working child actor to teen actor to adult actor, and almost no one *should.* There would be no incentive to work hard and improve if it were that easy!

"We run into that situation with children. Someone goes to LA and gets cast during pilot season, gets her SAG-AFTRA card, and now can't do anything. I wish they could just quit the union from age fourteen to eighteen," says Nora.

That's what Donna ran into, too. She basically quit the

business once puberty hit, both because she was getting more into boys and less into theatre and because the roles just weren't there. Even for film and television work, there are too many eighteen-year-olds who can play fourteen and then the producers don't have to hire tutors and worry about running afoul of child labor laws. So any roles that actually exist for kids in those gap years are usually taken by young adults who look younger than their age.

Donna did school plays and eventually came back to the business in her last year of college when, on a whim, she went to an open call for *Saturday Night Fever* and booked it. She was on track to become a lawyer but decided to follow this path to see where it led.

"I was in the right place at the right time," she said.

She was cast in the chorus and began taking acting and dance classes with the money she earned. She waited tables for two years and then landed the first national tour of *Hairspray* and never looked back—she's been acting professionally ever since.

Schooling

Nowadays, most professional child actors are homeschooled, using online curriculums. To work legally, though, the child has to prove that they're performing on grade level and able to read and write. They also can't have a bunch of unexcused absences because of auditions beforehand. Children's auditions in New York City have to start after 3:00 p.m. to account for school hours, but of course out-of-town people may have to bail out of school a lot earlier to get there on time.

Consider strongly the pros and cons of homeschooling in this fashion. Both parent and child have to stay really committed to it to make it work; a few hours of schoolwork here and there are not going to be enough.

Performing Arts High Schools and Colleges

As I mentioned, I went to a performing arts high school that I loved, and then I went on to a conservatory. Both of them had a huge influence on my career.

My teacher at Virginia's Governor's School for the Arts, Alan Fischer, says that when you're looking at schools, you should pay attention to teachers, not the beauty of buildings. The most important factor in how much you'll get from your college education is how you click with your professors. Most programs for people wanting to go into musical theatre are four years long, whereas programs for classical singers are sometimes much longer. People studying classical music usually go on for a master's degree, which adds two years to their training, before starting their careers.

To choose my college, I toured several and paid for a voice lesson at each place with one of their teachers. I think it's very important to do this; you need to see if you're going to be a good fit with whoever will be your main voice teacher in the program. You should be able to gauge quickly whether or not your personalities work together and whether you feel you can get something out of this person's lessons. For me, it was the voice teacher at CCM, Donna Connelly, with whom I meshed the best.

From the start, she suggested mixing German arias with musicals like *Oklahoma!* and *Carousel* during my training, and I felt relieved that I didn't have to convince her that I wanted to study both opera *and* musical theatre. She understood me right away and encouraged me to pursue my goals, rather than trying to get me to pursue her goals for me.

The relationship you'll have with a voice teacher is personal. If you don't find someone who speaks your language on the first try, keep looking. You'll find the right match.

Child Stars

Even though lots of kids want to perform, it's well known that thrusting them into a business geared toward adults can lead to all kinds of problems that they're not mature enough to handle. When you think about how tough it is to deal with rejection as an adult, imagine that during the years before your self-concept has even formed. The applause is exciting, but the disappointments are really rough. And it's confusing to get into situations where they're competing for roles against other kids with serious ambitions and bragging to one another, in addition to all the complications of how to deal with schooling, money issues, being away from friends, not being able to go to birthday parties, and so on.

I highly encourage parents to support their kids' ambitions, but within a limit at those tender ages. Get them into lots of classes and workshops by professionals (like

Destination Broadway!), have them do local shows, and go to big auditions once in a while if that works for you. But they get only one chance at childhood, and you have to consider your family. New York can wait until after school is finished.

14

Avoiding Scams

Pick any creative field in the world and you can be sure that someone is out there trying to figure out how to take advantage of people who want to be in that field. Whenever there are earnest dreams involved, and high competition to achieve those dreams, scammers know there's an opportunity to make big promises and line their own pockets.

The acting world is rife with people who are all too eager to take your money.

One of the biggest scams you'll find relates to headshots. People posing as agents or managers will post ads saying they're looking for new talent. Some will even have free seminars where they tell you that they can find you acting work. They may have a few modest achievements to show you—like that one of their clients has worked as an extra on a television show or had a bit part in a movie. Or they may claim credits that aren't even theirs to claim—like when a former client of theirs went on to find a *real* agent and then had success, they might still say that they "discovered" that client, leading you to see them as more legit than they actually are.

What's going on most of the time is a kickback scheme. They'll tell you that they think you're just terrific, terrific, terrific but that you need more professional headshots. And they just happen to know a photographer who'll give you a discount.

The truth is that those types of agents are not in the business of making money by finding you work; their main source of income is as salespeople for photographers. Once they have your headshots, they will likely do nothing with them. Maybe they'll submit you for things you could just have easily submitted yourself, but more likely, they'll just walk away with the money they made from photographer kickbacks.

There are also phony agents and managers who charge fees for other miscellaneous things—a "setup" or "initiation" fee (always bogus), a fee to put you up on their website, a fee to create a website for you or submit it to search engines, a monthly fee for web hosting, a fee to make a demo reel for you, a fee for their own seminars and classes . . .

Some of these phonies will tell you that this is just because you're a beginner and that it costs them money to get your career off the ground. They convince you that you're just paying up front for them to submit your material to casting directors and that they'll reimburse that money from your first paycheck, or something similar. They'll make you feel like they recognize your talent and that this is a smart investment.

Real agents don't charge you anything, ever, except for the commission they take from your booked jobs. They may make recommendations for things like photographers or classes if you ask, but they never suggest that you must or even *should* work with particular people they know. There are no "discount codes" they give you for photography services (that's a sure sign they're tracking kickbacks). When dealing with agents and managers, the only place you should ever sign a check is on the back. They don't take your money before you've booked a job, period.

But what about . . .

Nope.

But there's this one thing that sounds reasonable . . .

Nuh-uh. I mean it. No up-front fees are legitimate. You don't need a publicist before you're a public figure. You don't need anyone to professionally tape your auditions. You don't need to front any kind of money for postage or copying or anything else. You *do* need to give your agent copies of your headshots, and they should be done professionally if you're over eighteen, but it's completely up to you to choose a photographer based on the style you like and your budget.

One of my friends got sucked in by these types of scams not once but twice when she was a teenager—once with a phony modeling agency that sent her to a specific (bad) photographer who charged about $400 for pictures that would never pass muster in the real modeling world, and then again by a "talent agent" who convinced her parents to pay for them to produce a "demo commercial" for Hallmark cards, with the idea that they would send it to Hallmark and somehow convince them to run it as is. That's not how anything works.

Over the course of a few sessions, they were taping a bunch of these demos for other major brands, so my friend got to watch a series of poorly written, poorly produced videos being shot. At some point, even though she was only a young teen at the time, even she realized that there was no way Hallmark or anyone else was going to buy these commercials. But her parents had already paid the production fee up front, an expensive learning experience.

Unsurprisingly, after the demo, neither my friend nor anyone else who was recruited to do these demo commercials ever heard from the talent agent again. He disappeared, likely to resurface under a different name. There are plenty of them around, advertising in classified newspaper ads and online. There are even "modeling scouts" in many malls, just out to make you feel excited that they noticed you so that you'll spend lots of money on their photos, pageants, and other schemes.

Real agents don't set themselves up at malls, and they don't need to advertise. You're not going to find them on Craigslist, or in Google ads, or in your local paper with too-good-to-be-true headlines like SEEKING NEW TALENT! ALL TYPES NEEDED! MAKE $500/DAY AS A FILM EXTRA! (Film extras do *not* make that kind of money!)

Agents with legitimate credits are so inundated with submissions that they don't have to pay to seek out new talent. When they're really looking for talent, they go to shows and showcases, or they update their submission guidelines on *Backstage*. Most agencies are open to finding new talent as long as you follow their policies about what and how to submit.

It's tough to admit you've been scammed, and sometimes it's very tempting to buy into it when a person shows great enthusiasm for your talent. *This person believes in me! He wants to give me a chance!* you may think. But having a bad agent is worse than having no agent at all. You don't want your submissions coming in from someone with a bad reputation or who will handle your material unprofessionally and submit you for things you're not right for. You don't want your own name and reputation being associated with anyone who's not aboveboard.

"NEW" AGENCIES

If you stumble upon someone whose agency name you can't find in reputable directories, there's a 99 percent chance there's a good reason they're not listed.

You may believe that the agent is just new to the business and that you want to give him or her a chance. But agenting isn't something you jump into from nowhere; you start out as an assistant or associate agent at a reputable agency and work your way up, most often. At the very least, you work in another capacity (producing, directing, performing) before switching over to agenting. Either way, all agents should be googleable. You should be able to find the person's history in the business pretty easily. Verify claims whenever possible; don't just trust the person when they say they've worked with tons of big stars. One of the ways people like this get away with it is that they know you likely can't just call up the big-name stars they mention, so they figure you won't be able to fact-check them. But someone claiming to have worked with major stars will have left a digital footprint ... unless by "working with" them, they actually mean they were parking their cars or holding their umbrellas.

A real new agency should get your attention only if it broke off from a different established agency. Sometimes partnerships split or different partnerships emerge, and then an agent at a well-known agency might start up a new agency. But again, that would be very easy to search online or read about in industry publications. An agency you've never heard of that has no digital tracks is not going to do anything to help your career and might even hurt you. Hold out for the real thing.

"I'll Make You a Star, Baby!"

Anyone who makes big promises is suspect. Real agents always hope that their potential clients have star quality, but they know better than to make it sound easy or to pump up their clients with false hopes. Most working actors are not going to be stars, but that's okay—they're still working actors!

They may also puff up how exclusive this invitation is or

make up fake statistics to tell you how selective they are—like that they only accept 5 percent of the people who audition for them. (Nonsense; they accept anyone who they think has money.)

The people who make big claims about stardom are usually selling something—their classes, their pictures, their publicity services, whatever. They drop big names and claim that they have all kinds of (unverifiable) connections, but in reality, they have no idea how to make you a star. They just know how to get into your wallet. Don't fall for it.

There are all kinds of variations on how they'll worm their way into making you pay. They may first have you attend a long seminar at a hotel where they make you feel special for being selected, and only after you've already invested the time and felt good about what they said about you do they bring up the $595 "portfolio fee" that they'll need to make you a star.

Or they may make you pay an up-front fee online but say that they'll refund it if you're not accepted into their exclusive program. Of course, everyone is accepted, so there are no refunds to consider.

On AuditionsFree.com, one dad tells a heartbreaking story about what happened after he heard a radio ad that offered the chance for auditions with Disney and Nickelodeon. He and his wife booked an appointment for their five-year-old daughter, and when they arrived, it was a packed seminar at a hotel with people of all ages. They thought that was strange, but they were soon sucked into the mystique: "This lady talks on and on about how she's from Paris, grew up in Nigeria, and her parents sacrificed their lives for her dream. It was all very professional, and we bought every drop of it. Then, this kid Zeke from *Wizards of Waverly Place* comes running down the aisle, exciting the kids and reassuring my wife and I that this is real! *They do have Disney connections!* were my exact thoughts. This kid talks about how many times he was turned down before making it and how his parents sacrificed everything for him after he heard a radio commercial for acting just as we did, giving the impression that he works and gets work through Casting Hub as well. Well, now we know that isn't true, either."

They got a call that night claiming that their daughter was one of the very few to be chosen for a callback early the following morning—which they later realized was so they wouldn't have time to do proper research before being told that the package would cost about $8,000 per year to give her access to national auditions (or the bargain price of $2,000 per year for local auditions only). Of course, there were sales pitches designed to get them to hurry up and buy right now, because there was an audition that she was just perfect for if she signed up *today.* And, the woman said, she believed in the girl so much that she would pay half the money out of her own pocket. The parents were taken in enough to fork over a check immediately—before doing research and realizing that the business had changed names numerous times (and would continue doing so for years to come), that there were complaints all over the internet about them, that local news stations said they'd also received complaints, and that the actor who was paid to appear at the seminar even admitted that he would not recommend paying them to represent anyone. ("I'd spend my money elsewhere" is what he told the father who wrote to him for reassurance.)

After the father posted about his experience, many others

posted about theirs—nearly identical experiences in major cities at major hotel chains across the United States. Late-night acceptance calls for early-morning callbacks after the seminar so there was no time to research. Always one child or teen actor featured at the seminar to give an air of legitimacy, even though the actor had never been represented by the agency.

Three people showed up to defend the agency, and you might have been confused at first glance . . . one very convincing mother, especially, said that her son had booked numerous jobs through this agency. The webmaster finally interjected to say that all three defenders, with different identities, were coming from the same IP address.

This is what you're up against as a naïve actor-in-training, especially as a child or teen. No matter what they say, no matter how they try to make it sound like a once-in-a-lifetime opportunity, the minute they ask you to pay for *anything*, walk away. It's always unethical and sometimes illegal.

Nigerian Princes

One of the current scams going around online is a takeoff of the Nigerian prince scam that's been around almost as long as the internet itself, but this time, it's targeted toward people who have posted on acting or modeling websites. A person posing as a casting director sends out emails offering a contract for an upcoming job. When the person signs and accepts, the phony casting director sends a large, bogus check—an up-front payment, he says, for wardrobe or travel or whatever other reason. Then he tells you to keep some of it and wire the rest somewhere (or put it in a bitcoin e-wallet).

The check takes a few days to bounce, and in the meantime, either you've wired money from your actual account to the scammer or they've gained access to your financial information (plus they have all your contact information from the contract you signed).

Always Google the name of any unknown person who contacts you with a job or audition offer, and never agree to wire money anywhere or deposit it in a weird account—there's no reason for you to ever send money to someone who's supposed to be hiring you! Unfortunately, there are a lot of these scams, and as long as people keep falling for them, they'll continue.

NO NUDES

Some acting jobs (mostly film) do require nudity. What they never require, however, is for you to send nude photos to the casting director online. This is always a scam and can cause your photos to end up in places you wouldn't want them to.

It's Not a Secret

Real agents and casting directors don't hide their identities. When you see an ad that says something like, A MAJOR CASTING AGENCY IS SEEKING MEN AND WOMEN AGES 18–35, ALL ETHNICITIES, FOR A FEATURE FILM. CALL NOW, just forget it. That's not how casting agencies work—they don't put out anonymous calls with vague criteria like this. They don't use liaisons to vet their submissions through mass media. Stick to the established channels that you know are legitimate, not radio ads, local newspaper classifieds, or the booth at the mall.

Definitely not the booth at the mall.

Casting Couches

Luckily, the "casting couch" epidemic that's still very real in the film and TV world is not prevalent in the stage world. Some of the casting couch stuff there does come from people who are legitimately working in the industry taking advantage of their positions, and some of it is nonsense—just random people claiming to have connections they don't actually have as a way to trick people into compromising positions. One of my friends answered an ad in a college newspaper seeking an actress for a promotional job but was rightfully concerned when the director asked her to meet him in a hotel. She brought a friend along for safety, and they quickly realized that this was not a legitimate job opportunity and he was instead trying to lure women up to his hotel room.

In the theatre world, there are very few promises that you could ever "sleep your way to the top," but the one thing you should be aware of is that theatre people can be very . . . free with their bodies sometimes. We tend to be a very open, huggy, touchy bunch, and for the most part, that works out just fine and everyone's on the same page. But there are people who don't have great senses of boundaries and who may make you feel uncomfortable, especially in dressing rooms or on tour, where a booty slap might mean, "You go, girl!" but could also make you wonder, *Why is this person touching my butt?!*

I feel lucky that I've never felt like someone took it too far—all of my experiences have been positive. If you ever do have a problem this way, though, you can always bring it up to the company manager. It is possible for lines to get crossed, and no one should ever make you feel unsafe or uncomfortable at work.

Real Opportunities

In this business, if something seems like a shortcut or seems too good to be true, it almost always is. It's hard to take a tough stance when you think someone is complimenting you and trying to help you achieve your dreams, but throwing away your money is not only unhelpful for you, it also perpetuates the scams. As long as these people know they can lure in more victims, they'll keep doing it.

Scammers don't have changes of heart; if you find information that says someone was a scammer years ago, he or she still is. Keep moving.

If this were an easy business to get into, there wouldn't be a market for scams. It's true that professional acting is competitive and that it may take time for you to get your career going, but stick with it and stay on the path. Real success is worth it.

15

You've Never Arrived

As I learned, being on Broadway was amazing! But almost as soon as I got there, my thought was, *What next?*

With that major goal accomplished, I didn't really know what was next on my horizon other than that I hoped to be in more Broadway shows. My agent encouraged me to start auditioning again quickly after I had landed my first role in *Wicked,* even though I had an ongoing contract, because of the unsteady nature of the business—you have to keep auditioning even when you have a gig because you need to keep those connections. You want creative teams to remember you, so you can't disappear for a year.

Here's what I didn't know would happen: at nearly every audition, the casting team's eyes would light up when they saw *Swing* on my résumé—I'd been a swing for both *Wicked* and *The Drowsy Chaperone*. Being a swing is a valued role in a production—it shows that you're capable of the requirements of that job, meaning that you can learn many parts quickly and keep them in your head. Usually that means you're a really good dancer, if it's a dance-heavy show, or a really versatile singer. But the downside of it is that you can become such a valuable swing that they don't cast you in principal roles.

Once you've done (or understudied) a part, you're much more likely to be invited back to do it again. For instance, I had left *Wicked* and was doing tours and symphonies for a while, and then I got a call asking if I'd take over a particular role in the ensemble because someone needed six months off to recover from surgery. I'd covered that track before as a swing, so they knew I could pick it up quickly again, rather than holding an audition and starting from scratch with someone else. This was part of the reason I did *Wicked* on and off for ten years; there were many opportunities to come back because they knew I could pick up nearly any female part at any time. It took seven auditions to get there, but once I was in, I was in for good. Broadway is not geared toward giving new talent a chance; it's meant to be efficient and profitable. Reusing people who've played the role before means less rehearsal time and fewer costume expenses.

There are even *universal swings* whose job it is to fly wherever they're needed at the moment: Broadway, the national or international tour, the San Francisco sit-down, the Chicago sit-down . . . it's a tough job.

After auditions, I was invited to be a swing in *Mary Poppins* and in *Young Frankenstein*.

My gosh, this is incredible! I thought—at first. It was such an honor to be offered roles in multiple Broadway shows. But then I had to consult with my agent and think about what accepting those roles would do for my career.

Really, what it would do was solidify the idea that my destiny as an actress was to play a swing.

Being a swing was an exciting challenge, and believe me when I say I'm not complaining about getting cast that way—but I didn't want it to be my final stop. I had dreams beyond the ensemble, and I began recognizing that the more times *Swing* or *Dance Captain* appeared on my résumé, the less likely it would be that anyone would see me as a lead actress. I felt like I was on a hamster wheel.

Adding variety to my résumé wasn't worth the trade-off of leaving my dream show and keeping the same title that might, in the end, be an anchor on my career. I spoke with the *Drowsy Chaperone* director about it, and he had a simple suggestion for me: Leave it off the résumé.

"You were also my Janet understudy," he said. "Just say that."

It was a bit of a revelation, this idea that I didn't have to tell all. After some more time in the business, I began recognizing that you have to direct your career in the way you want it to go, and that means that once you've determined what your brand is, you start leaving behind anything that doesn't fit your brand—both in real life and on your résumé.

I've also been in the Miss America pageant, and along with some of the other things on my résumé, I knew it looked like all I knew how to do were lighthearted roles. So now I have a few different versions of my résumé where I showcase different things and leave others off.

There are times when you won't have much of a choice in

what roles you go out for because you just plain need a job, but when you do have any say in the matter, start being more selective. You want opportunities to show that you can handle the roles you want. A résumé filled with ensemble roles in Broadway shows or national tours means you'll probably get viewed as an ensemble member. A shorter résumé that shows a couple of your ensemble roles but also lead roles in regional or community theatres may set you on a better path, even if the pay is not as good or the work is not as ongoing.

The more times you accept a role that doesn't really fit what you want or where you want your career to go, the more likely it is you'll keep heading on the wrong path. Sometimes it's smart to take the risk of turning down a "sure thing" and waiting for the dream role instead, as long as you have a financial cushion.

Over time, I did achieve my goal of moving on from swing and ensemble roles and playing the principal role I'd always wanted, both on national tour and Broadway. I honestly thought that, with that on my résumé, I'd have lots of doors open for me at the end of it.

That wasn't the case.

So many times, I found out about a role I thought would be great for me and asked my agent to submit me for it, only to hear back that I couldn't get an appointment. It was demoralizing, and it reminded me again of a saying we have in this business: You've never arrived. Or, as basketball player JJ Redick adds, "You've never arrived. You're always becoming."

My friends and I even had an ongoing joke: *#can'tgetseen*. Now, as you build up your relationships and prove yourself through your work, it does become much more likely for you to remain a working actor, but it's not a business where the people on top stay on top, unless you hit the level where you have mainstream fame (like Sutton Foster and Kristin Chenoweth) and your name alone can sell tickets.

Each new creative team has their own preferences and prejudices, and sometimes the roles that are available on the biggest shows just aren't roles that fit you. There are lots of singing waiters and waitresses at Ellen's Stardust Diner in New York City who are "between" Broadway shows, waiting for another big shot to come their way—and serving cheeseburgers between songs in the meantime. Or performing as costumed characters at kids' birthday parties, or trying out for roles in feminine hygiene commercials.

In my downtime, I have found other ways to keep my career active. As I've said, I do lots of symphony concerts, *Cheek to Cheek* with Michael McCorry Rose, regional theatre, and I teach—I have discovered how much I love teaching master classes to young people in particular. It's fun to see the enthusiasm and talent in the next generation and to be able to help them improve. I always try to present a realistic picture of the business, though, so that they (and their parents) will understand what it's like.

Here is one of the best examples of what I mean by this: A dear friend of mine, who I met on the tour of *Wicked*, Peter Ermides, played the title role of Tommy in *The Who's Tommy* on Broadway. He took over the role from Michael Cerveris. Peter is an amazing talent.

"One minute you might be starring in a leading role and the next you're supporting. Both are wonderful, because it has to be about the work," he told me. "The business is full of ups and downs and sometimes you're playing a principal and the next you're covering. But you go where the work is."

When I moved out of New York, he then confided in me that he was questioning how he felt about the business.

"As I've gotten older, I prefer to have more consistency in my life. Not knowing what's next is tough to deal with, but loving the art makes it so worthwhile . . . that's why I stick it out."

Peter and I agree that this business can have a way of toying with your confidence. You are not going to get every role you audition for, even when you feel it was the best audition you've ever had. That's when it can weigh on you.

"I find it important to take classes and stay in classes to be challenged and be around other artists who are creating. It pushes me to keep growing and keeps me on my toes."

There's almost no other job quite so apt to mess with your self-esteem on a regular basis. Normally, if you're good at your job, it's pretty simple to tell. You get work; you keep work. Here, it's so easy to think, *Maybe I'm not that good. Maybe that one casting director liked me but no one else will. Maybe I'm a one-hit wonder. Maybe I'm not as good as So-and-So. Maybe I'm not attractive enough* . . . On the one side, it keeps you humble, but on the other, it can be too much.

Some of my lowest moments of insecurity were in front of casting directors who were younger than I was. I would think, *Am I cool enough?* I've walked in the room and wondered how these young people in power saw me, and the question ate at me until it messed up my audition. Later, I would think, *Why do I care if they think I'm cool? I'm not looking to go out to lunch with them . . . I'm looking for a job.*

If only there were a certification, like in teaching, that you could hold on to or tack up onto your wall to remind yourself, *I* am *qualified for this job.* But the best you can do is just to remind yourself that everyone goes through it. All performers have good times and dry spells. All performers have times when they think they've finally made it—only to learn that it's still a grind the next time they need a job.

Leaving the Biz

I have had friends who've left the business, and at first I felt sad for them. I felt like they'd given up. But time has given me another perspective, and that's that it can be a perfectly healthy decision to move on and find another career. It doesn't mean you have to give up performing altogether, but it means you give up the idea of making it your main source of income.

I'm happy for anyone who's doing what they love. For some people, the stress of the business means they no longer love it the way they did when they were just doing it for fun and competing for roles only against their classmates or people around the local community. Other people come to realize after a couple of years that they're just not getting callbacks, or they're not at the level to compete professionally the way they hoped they were, and they go off in search of a different career where they can really shine and where the financial end of things isn't as insecure.

While I still don't believe in going into this field with a "backup career," that doesn't mean I think no one is allowed to change course after giving it a fair shot. I've always said and still believe that the only reason to be in this business is if you cannot imagine your life without it. There is nothing else on earth I want to do more than perform, so I'm going to keep doing it! My life feels like it wouldn't be complete without it. For me, the positives outweigh the negatives, but that doesn't mean that it feels that way for everyone. We all have our own paths in life, and performing may be your lifetime career or just a stop along the way to something you like even more.

16

The Show Must Go On

No matter what disasters and stressors happen in your life, you can't bring it to the theatre.

Real life is messy. Things happen that you wish would never happen; people and pets you love die, your health takes a nosedive, your apartment floods and you lose irreplaceable mementos . . . all kinds of things happen that you have to deal with without letting it affect your rehearsals and performances. When you have a desk job, you may be able to sit there miserably without anyone noticing, but on stage, you still have to come across completely engaged and enthusiastic about whatever it is your role calls for. You can't bum the audience out with your sadness or stress—they come to the theatre to escape from all that!

I've had many challenges throughout my theatrical career,

but probably none worse than the one I faced when I came back from tour.

Art Imitating Life

I was married to someone in the cast of *Wicked*. And, like some marriages don't work out, this one didn't. I was absolutely devastated. I didn't want to tell anyone what was happening—how do you admit that your picture-perfect life has just shattered? But there it was.

The reality was that I had to go to work every day and put on a first rate performance, with him in the same building of course, notwithstanding the emotional roller coaster I was on.

The stage manager came by a couple of times to check on me during the early performances.

"You're such a professional," she said. "With all that you're going through, you've never brought it to work."

I'm bringing it to work every day, I thought. But it meant a lot to me that she could see the effort I was putting in to keeping my personal "stuff" aside and continuing to serve our audience. That's what you have to do.

At that time, it felt like the worst thing that could have happened. And that's the kind of thing you have to contend with when your job is performing. Whatever life throws your way, you need to force it off to the side for those few hours and do your best no matter what. You're a performer and your audience is coming to be entertained.

Emergency Surgery

Another time, when I was the standby Glinda, I confided in my friend Donna Vivino, the standby Elphaba, that I'd been having terrible gas pain. I'd taken a whole bottle of Gas-X in about three days.

"You have to go to the urgent care place on the corner," she said.

"Oh, I'll be fine," I said.

"No, I'm serious. I'll go with you after the show."

I thought I was just humoring her, but I wound up rushed to the hospital to get an appendectomy straight from the urgent care center.

I owe her so much; if I'd kept waiting it out and trying to power through as always, it would have burst and been a much more complex problem that could even have been life-threatening. In my case, we caught it just in time, and they just had to remove my appendix. Donna stayed with me and texted one of the stage managers to let them know what was happening.

I soon found that I was a minor celebrity among the medical staff, many of whom were excited to take selfies with Glinda. One of the doctors who was there just as I was about to go under anesthesia began singing the lyrics to "Defying Gravity" with such earnestness. He even did the spoken parts.

"Glinda, come with me. Think of what we could do . . . together!"

Despite my agony, I burst out laughing.

"Too much?" he asked.

It was such a painful experience, but the medical staff did their best to make it fun—and gave me a beautiful room.

My stage manager, however—the same one who'd told me earlier that she admired my professionalism—looked at things a little differently. Of course, that's her job.

The day after my surgery, she called. I thought she was calling to wish me well or check in. Instead, her first words were: "Tiffany, I haven't heard from you. You haven't called out. Are you coming or not?"

"I'm . . . in the hospital," I stammered.

"Yeah, I know, but I still have to hear from you."

"I'm sorry I didn't call."

"Honey, it's fine. It's fine. Obviously. I just have a ship to run here."

It was amazing to me. Outside of the theatre, this woman is my good friend. But one of the things I always noticed was how serious she was about her job and how everyone is equal inside the theatre; friends or not, she treated us all the same and expected the same high level of professionalism from all of us. Your call time is half an hour before the show, so 7:30 for an 8:00 show, according to union rules. When anyone signed in at 7:31, they were considered late. You didn't want to piss this woman off.

I thought it was pretty obvious that I wouldn't be in to work that day, considering that Donna had just told the company I had gone for surgery the day before, but the way the stage manager explained it later was that she needed to hear it from me. What if Donna said I wasn't coming, so she called in my understudy, and then I decide I've made a miraculous recovery and I show up? Or what if they don't know what's happening, so they hold up the show and then have to pay the whole crew overtime?

Short of your actual unconsciousness, you always have to

call—as early as possible, but no later than an hour before your call time. And even under the circumstances, she told me she needed me back in four days. The problem was that the main Glinda had a vacation that she'd already cleared a year in advance and the understudy had already cleared three or four personal days at the same time. My appendectomy was not very timely, but the show must go on.

Once people clear their dates, no one can force them to come back, so if I didn't show up, they were going to have to try to find an emergency replacement. Usually that would mean calling the Glinda standby from the national tour and paying for her to fly in to New York overnight, or finding another Glinda who had recently played the role and wouldn't need more than one rehearsal to get back into it. It's a stressful situation for any stage manager to be in, and it can be complicated by any similar problems that might be happening on the tour. If they can't afford to lose their standby either, then what? It can be tough to find someone who's ready on the spot and not doing another show.

"As soon as you can start moving, I need you here at the rehearsal hall during the show to go through the motions and tell me if you can do it in four days or if I need to call in reinforcements," she said.

When I walked through the stage doors the next day, the stage manager called out, "Oh my God." She wasn't expecting me to be walking so gingerly and slowly. I was still very tender and delicate from the surgery and the anesthesia, and to be honest, I wasn't sure how well I would do playing the role so quickly—but I didn't want to let anyone down. Rather than calling out, I decided I would walk through it and see what modifications I might need.

On her advice, I got a girdle to protect my incision and keep me "held together," and we modified a few pieces of choreography so I wouldn't strain too much. I told my musical director, Adam Souza, that I was a little worried about taking big, extended breaths to support long notes, and he said he would make the sound department aware that they should turn up the level on my mic so I wouldn't have to push as hard. We also changed up the scene where Glinda and Elphaba are fighting and a guard puts his arm around Glinda's waist to pull her away—he grabbed my arm instead.

The show must go on. And it did.

Never forget this is a business. It's times like these that you remember how much of a business it is and how you have to have a strong constitution to deal with the pressures that will inevitably come up. Your first priority, of course, has to be to make sure that you're safe. I wouldn't have done the show if doctors told me I couldn't, and my stage manager wouldn't have wanted me to go on either. You always have to remember that you get to do what you love *because* it's a business that runs on a strict schedule and under strict parameters and rules, and you have to treat it like the job it is.

Sacrifices

Times like those reinforced for me the kinds of sacrifices we all make to be in this business. So many of us have this big dream about performing starting in childhood. It looks really fun and glamorous and exciting. I still feel lucky all the time that this is how I make my living, and I still love what I do. Getting to sing and dance and act and never use algebra again? Heaven! But it does make me want to warn up-and-comers that there are pressures in this business that don't exist in most other jobs.

Can you handle it? It's something to consider seriously. I know many actors with long careers who have learned how to handle life's hurdles and make it work, but I also know others who've walked away. I don't judge them for it. I don't look at it as if they've quit. I understand that the constant uncertainty about when a show will close or where your next check will come from, combined with the need to put on a smile and perform even under the most trying circumstances, combined with the crazy schedules that leave little free time on weekends and holidays to be with family and friends . . . all of it can add up and overwhelm a person. I think it's good to think it through as much as you can before you decide that this is going to be your life. Just understand that achieving your dream may have trade-offs.

When the audience rises to their feet and claps, it's not about you: It's about the character. They likely don't even remember your name at the end. To the audience, I wasn't Tiffany Haas; I was Glinda. Depending on your perspective, that might be a little sad, or it might be pretty cool.

There's a positive to playing a character, as I'm sure you know on some level. When you're deep in the emotional muck, having to show up at the theatre and enter a different reality and give it your all for a few hours can be a great escape. You're forced to change your perspective for a while, which can actually help you to get out of a funk. No moping on the couch in your pajamas for you! And fellow actors are usually a good-natured, fun bunch to be around, so it can help your mood just to be around them. In the end, I think that if you can handle the pressure and uncertainty, being a performer definitely has its emotional perks.

THE BALLET SLIPPERS

There's a photograph that always sticks with me when I think about what it takes to make it in this business: a ballerina's feet up on pointe. One foot is wearing her pink slipper, and it looks so perfect—just what the audience oohs and aahs over. The other foot is bare and shows the reality of what's behind the pretty, delicate picture: calluses; bandages; red, mangled toes; and medical wrap. Ballerinas are *not* wimps!

It's a great metaphor for the life of a performer. The audience isn't supposed to see all that. They come for an escape, to see the magic of a wonderful show. But almost none of us get there unscathed. Performing *is* fun, but it's not *all* fun. It *is* exciting, but it's also nerve-racking. It takes real work, real sacrifice, and some mangled toes (or appendixes) along the way!

17

Serving Your Audience

Think about some of the best performances you've ever seen. What do you remember about them?

It made me cry.

I could hardly breathe when she sang.

I stood up and screamed at the end.

I got goose bumps.

It made me think about my first love.

I wanted to go hug my friend.

When we are truly affected by a performance, it's because the talent has made us *feel* something. We tend to remember not the specifics of the notes or the words or the routines but our reactions to them.

That's what theatre is all about: making your audience feel something. You want to make them laugh or cheer, or break their hearts, or keep them on the edge of their seats waiting for the conclusion of a story that's gripped them. You want them to feel like they know your character and have strong feelings about him or her.

That's what gets their butts into the chairs—the opportunity to feel something, safely, without experiencing it directly themselves. It makes people feel more alive and more connected when they can get emotionally wrapped up in a story they see unfolding in front of them.

And you're an integral part of that.

Those audience members likely know nothing about you personally, beyond what they may see in your bio, but if you're doing your job right, then they don't see Fancy Pants Actor; they see the character. After the show is over, they still see you as the character. That's how you've imprinted in their minds.

If you want devoted fans of both your show and you personally, the best thing you can do is to smile and stay in a good mood (even if you're faking it) and do whatever you can after that show to extend the experience for any audience members who've stuck around. Make eye contact. Many of them will be nervous about approaching you, but they want to say, "Great job. I really enjoyed the show." Don't get too busy greeting your own friends or talking to your fellow actors to acknowledge the people who just want your attention for a few seconds.

And volunteer to do publicity for every show you're in.

Let the creative team know you're willing and able to make appearances and do interviews to help promote the show. I've gone on morning news shows, radio shows, and podcasts and been interviewed for countless newspapers and magazines to support shows I've been in. No one pays you for these types of appearances, and it can be a bit of a strain on your personal time—sometimes you'll need to be in full makeup and ready to perform a number from the show at 7:00 a.m. for a local news station, or drive in traffic to meet a reporter for lunch—but it can have positive effects on the show and your career.

The main goal is to get people to come to the show. As an actor, you may think that's someone else's job, but it's always in your best interest to contribute however you can to make sure the show is a hit. You have a responsibility to care for the show. Never forget that if people don't buy tickets, there is no show.

I was often the go-to girl for *Wicked* press events, which surprised me in the beginning, but one of the stage managers said she liked having me represent the show because I always had an "attitude of gratitude." I knew my parents would love hearing that their lessons had stuck!

When the producers go to cast their next show, do you suppose they'll call on the person who volunteered to help publicize the show or the one who refused to do anything outside of the contract requirements? Anything you can do to show that you're a team player and ready to help everyone succeed is a positive mark for you.

Talking to the Press

Often, reporters will want to know the inside scoop about a show, so you may want to think through and talk through any interesting casting stories or unexpected things that happened during rehearsals before you are put on the spot. The other main thing reporters want to know is whether or not everyone's having fun and enjoying being in the show. Of course the answer to this is yes . . . even if it's not completely yes. Audiences don't want to pay to see a show that the actors don't want to be in!

You may want to try a few practice interviews with friends. Tape them so you can see and hear yourself. See if you have any bad habits—commonly, things like saying "Um" or "Uh" too much (once or twice during an interview is no big deal, but you don't want to use too many filler words or it gets awkward to watch), playing with your hands or hair, talking too fast, or rambling off topic.

If the host doesn't give the details of the show (where, when, how to get tickets), be prepared to do so yourself. Have a quick summary of the show memorized if it's not a very well-known play, and think of a good reason or two why everyone should come see it. Is it a great date-night show? A family-friendly show? Something that will keep people laughing or get them up on their feet? Is the choreography spectacular? The costumes? Now's not the time to be humble or shy about it—make the audience feel like they'll be missing out if they don't show up.

If you're stumbling for an answer, it's okay to say, "That's a great question," while you think for a second, or gently redirect if it's something you're uncomfortable answering.

Social Media

As you build a following, it's likely that people are going to want to stay connected with you on social media. There's no requirement that you have to be active online, but if you are, it's nice to at least let fans know what you're up to from time to time and be willing to acknowledge their comments.

Be careful about what you post online, though. Just like people warn about other jobs, casting directors really may check out your online profiles to see what you're like before hiring you. Be aware of the impression you give off. Pictures of you getting drunk every weekend or fighting with online trolls isn't what you want to represent to someone who is considering hiring you.

Also consider that you may wind up doing things other than just performing, as I have; now I also have online pages devoted to teaching/mentoring and my handbag and cosmetics line. For those reasons, too, you want to be careful about the kinds of things you post online; portray yourself as a friendly professional and you're more likely to get support for whatever you do.

Finding Joy

You must approach this business with gratitude and humility. So many performers think it's all about them, and they're wrong. When you can turn around your mind-set and realize that your place in it is to help your audience have a transformative experience, then you will find true joy in performing, even when the road is tough and even when some days it feels like it's taking everything out of you to just keep trying. Even when it feels like you have to defy gravity.

This business requires so much perseverance and hard work, but I truly encourage you to stick to it and never give up on yourself if this is what your soul needs. If you can't picture loving anything else the way you love performing, then I believe you're meant for this career. Have faith in yourself, invest in your talent, and keep walking through those audition room doors. The risks are great, but the rewards are greater.

I wish you a long, fulfilling, joyful performing career.

From Linda and Jim Haas

Hi! We're Tiffany's parents, and we have a message for those of you who have young sons or daughters who are determined to pursue careers as performers. We know exactly how you feel and what you're going through. Your child sees this career as 90 percent the dream and 10 percent the reality. As parents, we see things quite the opposite: We're 10 percent the dream and 90 percent the reality. Here's part of our story and what we learned. We hope you can get a few ideas, save yourself some effort, realize that what seems like chaos is normal and to be expected, and even manage a smile or two at what we all go through.

While we as parents are thrilled our child is enthusiastic and excited about something, we also wonder about the chances for success. We look at our precious children and want to protect them from a life of being told no in audition after audition. While our daughter was going through all her nos in the beginning of her career, we heard about every one. She was in New York, we were home in Virginia, and we constantly thought about what she was doing and worried about how she felt.

At least she was always in pursuit of the next audition opportunity and was too busy to dwell on the last one. We were just waiting for the next phone call, trying to discern from "Hi, Mom" how things went. "Honey, you'll be fine. Just move on, you're getting great experience, prepare for the next audition, and hang in there" works pretty well for the first two or three post-audition phone calls. Not so much for audition number fifty or seventy!

So while we told her we weren't worried, of course we did have concerns. There are so many talented people in New York, and it was hard to hear her have to withstand so much disappointment. But we knew getting into this that she would also develop resilience and self-sufficiency if she chose to make this her career, which have ultimately been positive life lessons.

If you haven't figured it out yet, this quickly becomes an all-consuming family project. Having a child who wants to be an engineer, a forensic pathologist, or a nurse is not necessarily a family project—there is no mystery there. Not like the great mystery of pursuing musical theatre. And we're constantly trying to figure out if they should perform in lots of shows to get experience or take classes to get training. Is this a good voice teacher? What about that guy that wants to take headshots of our nine-year-old for a special price of $1,200? Is that a good idea, and by the way, what exactly are we going to do with a hundred professional headshots of a nine-year-old when she won't even look like that next year?

We drive to dance classes, rehearsals, and auditions, and we wait and wait. Homework in the car on the way home from rehearsals? Dinner in the car on the way from voice lessons to dance class? Not to mention spelling words in the car on the way to school in the morning? Yup, been there, done that. A scheduling struggle, for sure, but a joyous struggle. And as we think back, we wouldn't trade the journey for anything, and we'd do it all again.

Not really sure how these young folks get bitten by the bug. When Tiffany was three years old and people came over for dinner, they were getting dinner theatre whether they liked it or not. If you just smiled, you have one of these in your family, too. Don't waste your time trying to talk them out of it using logic, either. This is not a logical pursuit. Just enjoy the ride and be thankful your child is passionate about something positive. There certainly are worse things.

We believe one of our jobs as parents is to provide opportunities. Sometimes we delivered them on a silver platter, but there was always the understanding that all opportunities had to be enthusiastically embraced with a 100 percent commitment to take advantage of everything that was presented. As parents, we can help—we can do lots of the planning and legwork, but when it all comes down to it, your children must become responsible for their success and be willing to pay the price. For an eight-year-old, that price may be skipping the birthday party because he or she chose to be in a show. Maybe they miss the school dance or can't be in volleyball because they have after-school dance classes. Not huge prices to pay, but eventually the prices get a little steeper.

Providing opportunities does not mean doing everything for them. Yes, parents are a key component of success, but eventually success must become the responsibility of the one who wants to be the performer! And as parents, we must facilitate that and slowly but surely turn over the reins and the responsibility for success. We will never forget Tiffany's college showcase in New York at the end of her senior year at CCM. After the rehearsal for it, we were walking down Ninth Avenue together, and her phone rang. A man on the other end said, "I saw you in your rehearsal. I want to send you in for a replacement for ensemble in *Beauty and the Beast.* Be at Chelsea Studios at 2:30 tomorrow. It's on Twenty-third Street. Be prepared to dance. Bring an up-tempo song. If you get the job, I'll be your agent for it. Goodbye."

As soon as he hung up, we looked at Tiffany, and all these thoughts went through our minds. *Did you write that down? Do you know how to find Chelsea Studios? Where are your dance shoes? What song are you going to sing? Do you remember that man's name?* The reality of what had just happened hit us over the head. We were heading home to Virginia the next morning, and this was not about us anymore. Tiffany was now living in New York, and success or failure was all riding on her from now on. We think part of our job as parents is to prepare our child (and ourselves) for that day.

This "family project" is a wonderful and hopefully joyous one, but still a bit of a mystery. The more you know, the less of a mystery it is. As Tiffany gained experience and did what she set out to do all along—have a successful performing career—we had lots of other parents approach us to ask for advice. *How did she do it?* Could their kids do it, too? So about fourteen years ago, we decided we should create a one-week summer teaching intensive for aspiring young performers and their parents. Our goal was to help them understand what's important and what's not, expose them to professionals in New York, help them develop a plan, and create an environment where these young folks can make the commitment that's so important to success as a performer. So far, nearly 1,450 talented young people from all over the country have attended this program. It's called Destination Broadway (www.destinationbroadway.org), and we hope you'll check into it if you have a child between eight and eighteen who's serious about performing.

Being a theatre parent can be nerve-racking, but it's also exciting. When you get to see your child take a bow on a Broadway stage for the first time and you still picture that little girl in the Annie wig in your living room dreaming about this day, it gives you a feeling of pride and joy that's hard to match in this life. We hope you will have the same kind of terrific journey.

Glossary

Apron: The area of the stage in front of the curtain and closest to the orchestra pit.

Breakdown: A description of the characters in a show, used for auditions.

Call time: What time you're expected to be at the theatre.

Company manager: The person in charge of payroll, contracts, housing (if applicable), and final approval of personal days.

Dark: When a show is off for the night (or day). Monday nights are usually "dark" on Broadway.

Dry tech: The first technical rehearsal, done by the crew without actors.

ECC: Equity Chorus Call (an audition for ensemble roles).

EPA: Equity Principal Audition (an audition for principal roles).

Front of the house: The box office, lobby, and audience seating—and the name for the staff who work in those places (like ticket sales agents and ushers).

Full beat: With makeup and hair done as it will be for the performance.

Full dress: Rehearsal in full costumes.

House: The auditorium where the audience sits.

ITR: In the room (the audition room). When someone asks online, "Who's ITR?" they're asking which creative team members are at the audition.

Nontraditional casting: Casting ethnic minority actors, women, older actors, or actors with disabilities in roles where those things are not germane to the story. Has also been called *colorblind casting*.

Off-book: The *book* is the script. Being *off-book* means you have your lines memorized and you don't need to hold the script.

Open call: Anyone can show up to audition, Equity or non-Equity.

Put-in: The final rehearsal where a new cast member joins an existing cast.

Reel: Your demo tape, showing excerpts from work you've done on camera.

Repertory theatre: A cast that has more than one show ready to perform so they can alternate between shows.

Sides: The piece of the script you're expected to learn for an audition. This could be just a few lines or a few scenes.

Sitzprobe: German for *seated rehearsal,* it's the first rehearsal with the cast and orchestra, running through without any staging.

Slate: Your introduction at an audition (taped or in person). This may include (but won't usually include all elements) your full name, age (if under eighteen), height, where you're from, which part you're trying out for, and your agency. Can be used as a noun (your *slate*) or verb ("We want you to *slate*").

Swing: An actor who learns all the ensemble tracks and can take over for any of them as needed.

Track: A cast member's role or roles during the show (e.g., an ensemble member may play a shopper in one scene, a party guest in another scene, and so on).

Type-out: When a casting professional eliminates auditioners just based on appearance or résumés.

Wet tech: The first technical rehearsal that includes actors.

Index

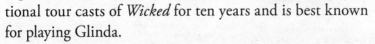

About the Authors

Tiffany Haas (www.tiffanyhaas.com) is a Broadway performer, concert vocalist, designer, and passionate entrepreneur. Throughout the years, her evolving career has spanned theatre, symphony concerts, and pageants, and sharing her many talents with others through teaching.  She was in the Broadway and national tour casts of *Wicked* for ten years and is best known for playing Glinda.

KRISNA GOODWIN PHOTOGRAPHY

Jenna Glatzer (www.jennaglatzer.com) is an award-winning writer and celebrity coauthor whose works include authorized biographies of Céline Dion and Marilyn Monroe. Her books have been featured on *The Oprah Winfrey Show,* *The Today Show,* and *Entertainment Tonight,* and in publications including *People* and *Time* magazines.

TARA LEE ALVES